JESUS' SCHOOL OF LIFE

Christoph Cardinal Schönborn

JESUS' SCHOOL OF LIFE

Incentives to Discipleship

Edited by
Hubert Philipp Weber

Translated by Michael J. Miller

IGNATIUS PRESS   SAN FRANCISCO

Original German edition:
Christoph Kardinal Schönborn
Die Lebensschule Jesu: Anstöße zur Jüngerschaft
© 2013 by Verlag Herder GmbH, Freiburg im Breisgau, Germany

Cover art:
Greek orthodox icon depicting Jesus (shown twice)
and his apostles on Lake Tiberias
©DPA/LANDOV

Cover design by Roxanne Mei Lum

© 2016 by Ignatius Press, San Francisco
All rights reserved
ISBN 978-1-58617-907-6
Library of Congress Control Number 2014944000
Printed in the United States of America ∞

*Dedicated
to the parish priests
of the Archdiocese of Vienna*

CONTENTS

Introduction   9

I.   "Become My Disciples"   13
      Jesus' School of Life
      The Master Plan—Jesus' Plan for Us   13
      Conversion as a Way   16
      Faith in the Messiah   19
      "Come Follow Me!"   21
      Discipleship and Self-Denial   24

II.   "But You Follow After Me"   26
      How Does One Become a Disciple of Jesus?
      The People of God from Abraham down to Today   27
      Jesus Calls Disciples   31
      Jesus' Family   34
      Is Everyone Called to Discipleship?   38

III. "Lord, Teach Us to Pray"   44
      Jesus' School of Prayer
      Getting to Know Jesus   44
      Jesus' Prayer   47
      Prayer to the Triune God   50
      The Spirit Prays in Us   56

IV.   "But I Say to You ..."   59
      The Sermon on the Mount as Jesus' School of Life
      To Whom Is the Sermon on the Mount Addressed?   62
      The Torah of the Messiah   65
      Jesus Himself Is the Torah   69

V. "I Came to Call Sinners"   76
    Is Jesus' School of Life Only for the Righteous?
    "He Will Save His People from Their Sins"   79
    The Forgiveness of Sins: The Heart of Jesus' Mission   80
    What Is Sin?   84

VI. "He Who Does Not Take His Cross ..."   91
     The Cross: The Key to Jesus' School of Life
     Love the Cross   92
     Love for the Crucified One   97
     The Cross and Self-Denial   101
     Affliction and Suffering   105

VII. "Go into All the World"   107
      Pupils Become Teachers
      The Whole Teaching of Jesus   107
      The Power of the Proclamation   111
      Simple Faith   113
      Teachers Are Witnesses   122

VIII. "Where Two or Three Are Gathered in My Name" 124
       The Holy Spirit as Interior Teacher
       The Spirit as Helper   125
       Remembrance of God's Deeds   128
       The Spirit Gives Witness to Christ   134
       The Holy Spirit Convicts and Convinces   136

IX. "I Am with You Always, to the Close of the Age"   140
     On the Way to Our Final Destination
     Eternal Reward   141
     Body and Soul   145
     Prayers for the Dying   148
     Passion for God   152
     Light and Shadows   154
     Impossible for Men, but Possible for God   155

Scripture Index   159

INTRODUCTION

"Lord, to whom shall we go?" After the discourse on the bread from heaven in the synagogue of Capernaum, many went away and no longer followed Jesus. Christians have this experience again and again, especially when they ask about the future of the Church. They often hear Jesus' question: "Will you also go away?" And Simon Peter's answer is: "Lord, to whom shall we go? You have the words of eternal life" (Jn 6:67–68).

The Archdiocese of Vienna is in an upheaval, like many dioceses throughout the world. Social conditions are changing, society is being transformed, and the Church needs renewal. For this purpose, Cardinal Schönborn started the program *Apostelgeschichte* (Acts of the Apostles) in Vienna. One essential element is the training of disciples. Before structural questions can be addressed, it is important to ask: What does Jesus Christ want of us? He calls us to follow him, to learn of him. But how does that happen? How can someone become a disciple of Jesus? This book originated from this situation. In the academic year 2011–2012, Cardinal Schönborn gave a series of catecheses on this question, which form the basis of this book.

The talks are quite scriptural, starting out from the Gospels in particular. They show how the way of conversion began in Jesus' school of life. And from this perspective the question arises: What does it look like today?

The course of the catecheses is also an adventure in search of the Lord's command. Anyone who gets involved with Jesus and his instruction sets out on a path of adventure.

Ultimately it is about great alertness and watching the signs of the times. What is God showing us in this time, in the realities among which we live? When we convert to the Lord, then not only the Church changes but society as well. The book intends to trace this path through nine stages:

What is Jesus' plan for us? The first chapter shows that the prerequisite for discipleship is faith in him, in Jesus, the Messiah, the Son of the living God. Faith means surrendering oneself entirely to Christ, converting, and walking in his ways.

No one can become a disciple on his own. Chapter 2 explains how discipleship begins with vocation. Jesus calls all men to follow him and thus builds up his family, the Church.

Chapter 3 looks at Jesus' school of disciples as a school of prayer. First the disciples learned from Jesus how to pray; indeed, they were fascinated and moved by his prayer. But this also shows the limits of prayer. Our prayer is weak unless the Spirit himself prays in us, as Paul says.

The Sermon on the Mount proves to be the charter of Christian living and discipleship. Chapter 4 is devoted to it. But does not the Sermon on the Mount make excessive demands? After all, who can love his enemies, always turn the other cheek, and go far beyond what is usually required in keeping every commandment? In the Sermon on the Mount, Jesus demands something of his listeners: ultimately, himself. For it is about being conformed more and more to him, the Son of God.

Jesus, however, calls no perfect disciples but, rather, sinners to follow him. Therefore chapter 5 asks about this call to sinners. What is sin in the first place, and what does it mean that we men are all entangled in sin? Sin, however, was taken away by Jesus, the Lamb of God, who died on the Cross.

Chapter 6 is dedicated to the cross as the key to Jesus' school of life. The cross alarms and frightens us. And yet there can be no path to resurrection that does not lead by way of the cross, and so no discipleship is possible that tries to get around the cross.

Chapter 7 describes how the students themselves become teachers, how they are supposed to witness to Jesus' teaching and hand it on. It is anything but obvious that there is a doctrine of Jesus that can be expressed in set formulas, since the content of the proclamation is Jesus himself. The disciples are supposed to tell about him and proclaim him.

Chapter 8 shows that the disciples are not left alone in their work of proclaiming Jesus. Christ sends the Holy Spirit as their counselor and teacher, as John tells us. Only in the power of the Spirit is proclamation possible.

Finally, the last chapter turns our attention to our final destination. Is there such a thing as a reward for discipleship? Eternal life, which is rarely mentioned today, is promised by Jesus as the reward for discipleship.

This, however, is not about a consolation prize but, rather, about a certain attitude. The Second Vatican Council says that the Church in this world is on pilgrimage toward her final encounter with Christ. And so being a disciple of Jesus means always being on the move in this world.

The Church, then, can walk safely along this path if she attends the school of the Master, in other words, if she learns from Jesus how she can live out the Gospel in this world. Only then will Christians remain true to their vocation in the future, too.

The Editor

I

"Become My Disciples"

Jesus' School of Life

When Peter remonstrates with the Master for announcing that he will suffer and be killed, Jesus says to him: "You are not on the side of God, but of men" (Mt 16:23). If we want to be disciples of Jesus, we must go to the school taught by Jesus himself so as to have the same mind as God and not cater to what people want.

The Master Plan—Jesus' Plan for Us

Jesus, the Master, our Lord, has a plan for us, a "Master Plan". If we do not carry it out, our efforts are in vain. "Unless the LORD builds the house, those who build it labor in vain", it says in Psalm 127:1. But who tells us what his plan is for us and for the Church today?

I wrote in my pastoral letter for the Fourth Sunday of Easter, May 15, 2011,

> By 'Master Plan', I do not mean a set formula th[
> carry around in my pocket. It is a matter of r
> asking the Lord himself, in a fresh, new way

What do you want us to do? The Church is not an end in herself! What are you telling us through the many people who are seeking? How do you allow us to hear your heartbeat in the lives of so many individuals who are not regular members of our congregations? Do you not want to lead us to rethink, to repent? Are you not calling us to line up behind you again, so as to follow you? Do we not all too often think in all-too-human categories, so that Jesus has to say to us forcefully, as he did to Peter: "You are not thinking of what God wants but of what people want" (cf. Mt 16:23)? Self-critically, I ask myself: Am I not secretly dreaming of the form of the Church that I experienced in my youth? Am I not secretly hoping that somehow we will succeed in winning back respect, acceptance, popularity, and tangible success for the Church? Am I really ready to say Yes to the present situation, to see it as the opportunity that God is giving us today? I am certain that Christ wants his Church to serve him as a sign and instrument of union with God and the redemption of mankind (cf. Vatican Council II, *Lumen gentium* 1). If the sign becomes unclear and the instrument useless, it must be forged anew, in the fire of trials, under mighty blows and in the silent melting of the material and the molding of it into its future form. For the Spirit wants to renew our hearts and, with them, the face of the earth.

We should think as the Lord thinks and not seek to put our own ideas into practice. "My thoughts are not your thoughts, neither are your ways my ways", we read in the Prophet Isaiah (55:8). I see as our first and most important task, in this time of upheaval and reorientation, the question: What does the Lord want? One thing we can say with certainty: He wants our life, our happiness. "I came ʼat they may have life, and have it abundantly", Jesus says

(Jn 10:10). "As the Father has loved me, so have I loved you; abide in my love.... These things I have spoken to you, that my joy may be in you, and that your joy may be full" (Jn 15:9, 11). He wants us to have happiness, life, and joy. And he shows us the way to it: "I am the way, and the truth, and the life" (Jn 14:6). That is the reason for his invitation: "Become my disciples" (cf. Jn 15:8).

To be a Christian means to become a disciple of Jesus. The Greek word *mathetes* literally means "pupil". Come to my school of life. "Learn from me; for I am gentle and lowly in heart" (Mt 11:29). At the conclusion of the Gospel, Jesus gives the Great Commission:

> "Go therefore and make disciples [literally: pupils] of all nations, baptizing them in the name of the Father and of the Son and of the Holy Spirit, teaching them to observe all that I have commanded you." (Mt 28:19–20)

Jesus' commission is to win people for his school of life. When he gives this commission, he wants us first to go to his school of life ourselves. That is a lifelong task.

How far along are we in this school? How are we Christians doing in the subject of discipleship? In his farewell discourse at the Last Supper, Jesus says: "By this my Father is glorified, that you bear much fruit, and so prove to be my disciples [pupils]" (Jn 15:8). Are we Christians actually Christians? One of the early witnesses, Saint Ignatius of Antioch, who died a martyr's death in Rome around the year 107, wrote a letter to the Christian community in Rome shortly beforehand. He was a prisoner en route to Rome and was to be thrown to the wild animals in the circus there. He feared that the faithful would prevent him from doing so and attempt to have his death sentence revoked. He wrote to them: "Let me be thrown to the animals!" He longed to become "Christ's pure bread". "Then I will at last be a true disciple of Christ" (*Epistle of Ignatius to the Romans* 4:1–2). "Allow me to be an imitator of the suffering of my God" (6:3), and then I will finally be a Christian. To be a Christian means to be a disciple of Jesus. To become a Christian means to become a disciple of Jesus.

One thing is certain: we remain in this school of life for our whole lives. One never graduates from Jesus' school of life, not until we are definitively with the Lord. I still remember the feeling of happiness I had when I was done with school after final exams. One does not leave Jesus' school of life. Although Jesus addresses us as his disciples and pupils, he is not simply the Teacher; he is also the Master, the Lord. In this relationship of disciples to the Master, more is at stake than just learning things. What is at stake is my life, a living communion that becomes ever closer and ever deeper, until I become totally one with him, as he is one with the Father.

Conversion as a Way

In many areas of life we are facing major upheavals. In the financial world, in the business world, in environmental matters, there is a great restlessness. Whether you look at the financial crisis, the ecological crisis, or the demographic crisis, no one has prescriptions to remedy them. Recently someone gave me a poster for my office that reads: "I have no solution, but I admire the problem." I think that ironically fits our situation.

Then, too, the upheavals in the Church must not be regarded in isolation from the upheavals in society. They leave us at a loss in many respects. I am suspicious of anyone who offers patent remedies. One thing we know with certainty: we need reforms, new approaches. There is only one way out of the financial crisis, namely, that *we all* change our behavior and stop piling up debts and speculating with illusory promises of profit. And this is true about the Church's path of reform: it is first of all a personal path of conversion, certainly the personal path of as many people as possible. "The time is fulfilled, and the kingdom of God is at hand; repent, and believe in the gospel" (Mk 1:15). With these words Jesus begins his preaching. They remain valid for all times. They are about the kingdom of God, about the dominion of God.

We talk much too much about the Church herself. Again and again Pope Benedict XVI recalls a Chinese proverb: "He who looks at himself does not shine." A Church that is primarily concerned about herself has no radiance. The Church serves the kingdom of God. That should be central again, so that his dominion, his kingdom takes effect. The Council says at the beginning of the Constitution on the Church, *Lumen gentium*: "The Church ... is like a sacrament or as a sign and instrument both of a very closely knit union with God and of the unity of the whole human race" (*Lumen gentium* 1). The Church serves this union. She can do so to the extent that her members are closely united with God and with one another. Therefore, the primary thing is always that we go to Jesus' school of life, each day anew.

Questions about how the Church can again win more respect miss the essential point. It is not about that. Of course it is nice when the Church has a good reputation, but that is not her task. It is not about the Church's prestige, but about God becoming visible, about us Christians making Christ visible. And for that we must once again go to his school.

I wish to have a new eagerness to learn, a new passion for asking the Lord: What is it like to be a Christian? Help us to spell it out in a new way! I wish to have a love for learning at Jesus' school, a genuine curiosity to rediscover Christianity, which is ancient and yet so new. Whether Christianity remains alive among us, or revives, depends decisively on this passion. I see exciting new things coming, great difficulties, no doubt, but also great opportunities. In 1939 a Jesuit priest, Father Karl Prümm, published a book with the title *Christentum als Neuheitserlebnis* (Christianity as the experience of newness; Freiburg im Breisgau). He saw early Christianity as an experience of newness for human beings. It appeared in the world at that time as something new and was welcomed as such by many or else opposed. Today, too, being a Christian is more and more often experienced as a novelty. For many seekers, the encounter with the Christian faith, with Christ, becomes something quite new. But in order for that to happen, it is necessary that we ourselves, the "older" Christians, discover it anew. "Behold, I make all things new" (Rev 21:5), says Jesus at the conclusion of John's Book of Revelation. We can rediscover the newness of our old faith only through a new encounter with the Lord. I am betting on this renewal. Many critics object that this is spiritualizing the problem, that it fails to address the concrete questions sufficiently, that the specific reforms are not taken into account. But what could be more concrete? What changes reality more than *metanoia*, the conversion to which Jesus is calling us: rethinking, repentance? Jesus calls us to set out on this way of conversion. This is thoroughgoing renewal, even today. It starts with me, with you.

Faith in the Messiah

We are familiar with Jesus' drastic words to Peter: Get behind me, you Satan! Get out of my sight! You are thinking as men think and not as God does! (cf. Mt 16:23). Jesus never said anything harsher to the apostles than this. In this Gospel, Peter not only has the role of the first apostle but also stands for all disciples of Jesus as their representative. This is why each and every one of us is allowed to recognize himself in Peter. Immediately before this was the famous scene at the source of the Jordan near Caesarea Philippi, when Jesus asks his disciples what people were saying about him and then asks them directly: "But who do you say I am?" The answer that Peter gave at that moment is famous: "You are the Christ, the Son of the living God!" Rightly did Pope Leo the Great (d. 461) and many Fathers of the Church say that this profession of faith is the rock on which the Church stands. This profession is also the basis of our discipleship. Without faith in Jesus, the Messiah, the Christ, one cannot be a disciple of Jesus. One can be an admirer, one can find him interesting, study him, regard him as a prophet or as the founder of a religion, but one can be a disciple and go to his school of life only if one really believes in him. Faith is therefore the first prerequisite for discipleship.

On account of this profession of faith, Jesus called Peter blessed. "Blessed are you, Simon Bar-Jona! For flesh and blood has not revealed this to you, but my Father who is in heaven" (Mt 16:17). We have here a critical foundation for Jesus' school of discipleship. Faith is the prerequisite. But this faith is a gift. God gives the gift of faith. Jesus would later make that clear when he said to his disciples: "You did not choose me, but I chose you" (Jn 15:16a).

After Peter's profession of faith, Jesus makes him a great promise with tremendous significance: "You are Peter, and on this rock I will build my Church, and the gates of Hades [that is, the powers of the netherworld or, as older translations say, the gates of hell] shall not prevail against it" (Mt 16:18). Then comes the promise: "I will give you the keys of the kingdom of heaven, and whatever you bind on earth shall be bound in heaven, and whatever you loose on earth shall be loosed in heaven" (Mt 16:19). The promise cannot be any more magnificent. It applies to Peter personally, above all officially, as the chief shepherd to whom Jesus entrusts his flock. But we will see that essentially this promise applies to every man and woman among Jesus' disciples. This is perhaps what we must learn first and most of all in this school. This is the incredible demand that God includes in this package of being a disciple.

The saints witness to this, for instance, the Little Flower, Saint Thérèse of Lisieux (d. 1897). Her experience of discipleship was incredibly strong, and with her little way she encouraged all of us: We *can* go to Jesus' school. It is possible. I will cite a passage from her autobiography from the end of Manuscript C, where she dares to apply to herself the high-priestly prayer of Jesus in John 17: "Perhaps this is boldness? No, for a long time You permitted me to be bold with You. You have said to me as the father of the prodigal son said to his older son, 'EVERYTHING *that is mine is yours'* [Lk 15:31]. Your words, O Jesus, are mine, then, and I can make use of them to draw upon the souls united to me the favors of the heavenly Father."[1] We need encouragement in order to recognize what Christ expects of us. The Little Flower dared to make Jesus' prayer to the Father her own, so much so that she simply adopts Jesus' words and speaks as Jesus to God. What great power of discipleship and what authority!

"Come Follow Me!"

And what happened to Peter, as he was learning to become a disciple of Jesus but fumbled so badly at the same time? Immediately after Peter's profession of faith we read:

> From that time Jesus began to show his disciples that he must go to Jerusalem and suffer many things from the elders and chief priests and scribes, and be killed, and on the third day be raised. And Peter took him and began to rebuke him, saying, "God forbid, Lord! This shall never happen to you." But he turned and said to Peter, "Get behind me, Satan! You are a hindrance to me; for you are not on the side of God, but of men." (Mt 16:21–23)

Jesus speaks about his suffering and death but also about his Resurrection. All they heard was: suffering and cross. The Resurrection seems to be forgotten to this day. So it often happens in Jesus' school of disciples that when trials come we see the cross primarily but not the promise of

---

[1] *Story of a Soul: The Autobiography of Saint Thérèse of Lisieux*, trans. John Clarke, O.C.D. (Washington, D.C.: ICS Publications, 1976), 255–56.

the resurrection. Peter takes Jesus aside and objects vehe-
mently; literally it says: "He began to find fault with him,
to rebuke him": "God forbid, Lord!" Then a double neg-
ative in Greek, *ou me*: "Never ever shall that happen to
you!" Now I am translating literally: "But Jesus turned
around and said to Peter: Get behind me, you Satan. You
are a scandal to me", a stumbling block, an obstacle. "Get
behind me", he says to Peter: *hýpage opíso mou*: "Get out
of my way, do not get in my way, get behind me." This
is the very same expression that Jesus had used at the Sea
of Galilee, when he called Peter and Andrew away from
their fishing boat. He said: *Deute opíso mou*, "come follow
me" (Mt 4:19). Jesus is therefore reminding Peter of his
vocation. Remember how it was in the beginning, when
I called you! Does not Jesus say to us, too: "Remember
how I called you. Go back to the place where I called you,
right at the beginning. Do not oppose me, do not get in
my way, do not resist, but rather get behind me again as at
the beginning: Follow me!"

Then Jesus gives a reason for this: "For you are not
thinking *ta tou theou*—the things of God but, rather, the
things of men." You are thinking as men think and not
as God thinks. But is it really like that: If you follow after
Jesus, are you not allowed to be human? Is there such a
deep chasm between what is human and what is divine?
Humanly speaking, of course, Peter's views were all too
human and understandable.

Three motives of Peter are important for our school of
disciples. First, Peter does not want Jesus to suffer. That is
very human, quite correct: That should never happen.

This is the perfectly normal reaction of a man who does
not want his friend to suffer. A mother does not want her

child to suffer. One's attitude toward suffering is the key question of discipleship. Peter is for Jesus a Satan and a scandal because he gets in the way of his suffering. For the way to suffering is the way to resurrection.

Peter's second motive is quite understandable. It is disturbing how briefly Jesus was together with his disciples, at most three years. After that short time, it was much too early to lose him. They had left everything, their profession, their social status, and security, and set out with Jesus as itinerant preachers, and now he was leaving them. What would become of them? The prophet Jeremiah complains to God in deeply moving words: "You have deceived me [more literally: You have betrayed me], and I was deceived [or: I let myself be deceived]; you are stronger than I, and you have prevailed" (Jer 20:7). The prophet says: What have I got myself into with you? Part of the crises in discipleship is the feeling: What have I got myself into? Where is this way leading us? First he calls us, then he abandons us.

The third motive in Peter's objection again comes from the very human feeling: Lord, that cannot be what you meant! You just solemnly announced to me: "You are Peter and on this rock I will build my church", that is, my *ecclesia*, my congregation, my community, the renewed People of God. Now it is just starting, and you say that you must die. Is the work of building, which has scarcely begun, now going to end so terribly and abruptly? Today we are in a similar situation with regard to our discipleship. There is disappointment about the fact that apparently decline is coming instead of building. Human logic is on Peter's side. "You are thinking as men think." But Jesus' discipleship means rethinking, thinking as God thinks.

Discipleship and Self-Denial

In the second part of this section from the Gospel we hear a key statement about discipleship:

> Then Jesus told his disciples, "If any man would come after me, let him deny himself and take up his cross and follow me. For whoever would save his life will lose it, and whoever loses his life for my sake will find it." (Mt 16:24–25)

Again translating literally: "If someone wants to walk behind me". This is the very same expression that he used in rebuking Peter: "walk behind me". If someone really wants to do that, he must deny himself, take up his cross, and follow me. Self-denial is a key word in discipleship. What does self-denial mean? We know very well what it means to deny. Peter denied Jesus. "I do not know this man" (Mk 14:71). We know what it means to deny a friend. Adolf Schlatter (d. 1938), the great Lutheran theologian, says: Self-denial means that you say to yourself, I do not know you. Say what Peter said to Jesus to yourself. Deny yourself. "He who denies someone breaks off his friendship with him.... 'I know nothing about him and do not want to know about him', Peter said later when he denied Jesus. 'Say that to yourself', Jesus advises us. You must not listen to your own counsels or to what you desire for your happiness. Detach yourself from yourself." Deny yourself, take up your cross. "We manage to do both only when drawn by a love stronger than our self-love."[2] It is

---

[2] Adolf Schlatter, *Das Evangelium nach Matthäus: Ausgelegt für Bibelleser* (Stuttgart, 1961), 260.

a question of a stronger love. It is about the one who says: Follow after me. If our love for him is stronger, then we are ready to walk after him even at the cost of self-denial.

Jesus did not make it easy for us. He did not promise anything comfortable. He showed the way to happiness, love, and the fullness of life: "Whoever would save his life will lose it, and whoever loses his life for my sake"—which means out of love for me—"will find it" (Mt 16:25).

II

"But You Follow After Me"

How Does One Become a Disciple of Jesus?

Does being a Christian always mean being a disciple of Jesus? If the answer is Yes, what does it mean to be a Christian disciple? What, then, is discipleship? If being a Christian and discipleship are not to be equated, however, is there then, so to speak, a general and a particular way of being a Christian, one for the general public and one for very special Christians, the disciples? I was directly confronted with this question because of my vocation to the priestly and religious life. Is that a special call, or is it simply a call to be Christian, to follow Christ? Can one be a disciple of Christ in a perfectly normal way, without any special form of life, without entering the state of religious life or having a vocation to the priesthood?

After the Bible, the most successful book in all the history of Christianity has the title *The Imitation of Christ* (*De Imitatione Christi*). In German, the title is *Die Nachfolge Christi* (Following Christ). This work by Thomas à Kempis, which was completed in 1441,[1] has nourished countless Christians in their spiritual life. As a girl, Saint Thérèse

---

[1] Cf. Peter Dyckhoff, *Auf dem Weg in die Nachfolge Christi: Geistlich leben nach Thomas von Kempen* (Freiburg im Breisgau, 2004).

knew most of it by heart. It is quite clearly written, not for a special group of Christians, but rather for everyone. It is also read by everyone, far beyond the world of Christianity. Many famous Christians and many more unknown ones have drawn from *The Imitation of Christ* their nourishment for the journey of Christian life and used it as a guide.

Dag Hammerskjöld (d. 1961) was Secretary General of the United Nations. In his spiritual diary, there are many quotations from *The Imitation of Christ*.[2] This great diplomat wanted with his whole being and with his whole life to be a disciple of Jesus. But he was neither a monk nor a priest. *The Imitation of Christ* was for him one of the guiding stars of his life. Another example was Robert Schuman (d. 1963), the great politician, one of the founding fathers of a united Europe. His process of beatification is under way. He, too, drew again and again from the book *The Imitation of Christ*.[3]

Is being a Christian the same as being a disciple of Jesus? Yes, no doubt, and yet not exactly. What does Jesus himself tell us? What was the experience of the early Church? What is the Lord showing us with regard to this question through the events of our time?

The People of God from Abraham down to Today

How did men come to make the decision to join Jesus and for his sake to leave everything, their family, their

[2] Dag Hammarskjöld, *Markings*, trans. Leif Sjöberg and W. H. Auden (New York: Knopf, 1964), for instance, the entries on April 7, 1953, or July 29, 1955, as well as others.

[3] Cf. Gisbert Kranz, *Von Aschoka bis Schuman: Zehn exemplarische Staatsmänner* (Würzburg, 1996).

occupation, their house, their acquaintances, their familiar surroundings? At the same time we must ask ourselves what it was like for those who joined Jesus inwardly yet did not travel with him but stayed at home. Finally, Jesus himself poses the question: What about those who know nothing at all about Jesus? Can the large majority of mankind somehow be disciples of Jesus?

First of all, an important point: following Jesus, as presented to us in the New Testament, does not take place in a vacuum. Jesus cannot be understood without his prehistory. His mission and his commission cannot be separated from the mission of Israel; they are part of "the story of the gathering of the people of God from Abraham until today".[4] In his book *Does God Need the Church: Toward a Theology of the People of God*, the exegete Gerhard Lohfink examines the question of why there is Church in the first place and what the mission of the People of God actually is from its first beginnings to the present day. Jesus' mission is inseparably connected with the election of the Jewish people, the People of God. We cannot have Jesus without the Old Covenant. It is a history of callings, a history of being set apart and commissioned, a history of mission and empowerment. If we want to reflect anew on Jesus and on following him in our time, we must never separate him or us from the long history of the Old Covenant. If you tried to have Jesus without the Old Testament, it would be like violin strings without a sounding box. We cannot understand Jesus without Israel, the Chosen People.

Here we are, already at the beginning of our journey, at an important fork in the road. If today we want to

---

[4] Gerhard Lohfink, *Does God Need the Church? Toward a Theology of the People of God* (Collegeville, Minn.: Liturgical Press, 1999), viii.

understand anew our commission as disciples of Christ, then we have to look at the journey of the Jewish people. That is our prehistory, those centuries of practicing a journey with the will of God. That is to say, practicing what it means to bear the yoke of election, as the Jews used to say. For Catholics in countries in which for a long time we were accustomed to being an often comfortable majority, it is a difficult learning process to adjust to a new situation in which practicing Christians find to a great extent in their surroundings, in their profession, in their circle of friends and colleagues, that they are a minority, even if the majority of the population here in Austria and in many parts of Europe identify themselves as Christian or Catholic. A Jewish acquaintance of mine accompanied me to the airport in Israel. On the way we talked about the situation of the Church in Austria. He asked me how things are, and I told him a little about the many people who leave the Church, the strong head wind that the Church in our country faces. Then, smiling, he said to me, "We have been used to it for centuries: whether you are likeable or unlikeable as a Jew, whether or not you win applause, one thing is certain: You are always a Jew! And consequently people look somewhat askance at you, at least in many parts of the world today that is still the case." And he said: "You Catholics will get used to it. 'Welcome on board', so to speak. Whatever you do, people will say, 'Tsk, tsk, the Church ...' Whether you have success or failure, whether you are criticized or praised, they will say, 'That Church, those Catholics ...'." This should not make us pessimistic but rather train us in what discipleship means, as Jesus understands it.

One remark by the great Jewish author and psychologist Manès Sperber, who lived in Vienna and mostly in

Paris, makes this clear. He writes in all seriousness in the first volume of his autobiography, *God's Water Carriers: All Our Yesterdays*, that few non-Jews have ever understood that suffering became the fate of the Jews, not in spite of their "chosenness", but primarily because of it. "By making a covenant with us, God threw the divine brick of his grace on us. Ever since, we have been enduring the oppressive burden of chosenness as a curse, and yet we are supposed to praise it as a blessing three times a day."[5] That is certainly a rather bitter way of putting it, but a serious and profound truth nonetheless. The yoke of election to Jesus' discipleship is in the tradition of the election of the Jewish people.

"If any man would come after me, let him deny himself and take up his cross and follow me" (Mt 16:24). This is the crucial point for the path of reform to which the Lord is inviting us: it is a matter of a new view of our Christian vocation. Gerhard Lohfink experienced this. He gave up his professorship at the university and joined a new Christian community. He writes:

> The Bible does not concern itself anywhere with pastoral plans and strategies. Instead, on almost every page it reveals that God does not act anywhere and everywhere, but in a concrete place. God does not act at any and every moment, but at a particular time. God does not act through anyone and everyone, but through people God chooses. If we do not come to recognize that again[,] there will be no renewal of the Church in our time, for this principle of salvation history is true today as well.[6]

[5] Manès Sperber, *God's Water Carriers: All Our Yesterdays*, vol. 1, trans. Joachim Neugroschel (New York: Holmes & Meier, 1987), 39–40.

[6] Lohfink, *Does God Need the Church?*, viii.

God acts through human beings whom he chooses. Are we among them? That was the question that I asked myself as a youth: Am I one of the ones who are chosen for a definite task, a definite mission?

Jesus Calls Disciples

How was it at the beginning? Jesus starts his public ministry by calling individual men and gathering them around himself. The Church is the gathering of people in and around Jesus. The first callings are depicted very briefly by Mark the Evangelist. Two fishermen, Simon and his brother Andrew, are at work. Jesus walks by on the shore and says: "Follow me and I will make you become fishers of men" (Mk 1:17). Jesus calls them authoritatively, quite definitely, and without discussion: Would you like to ... is this all right with you? Mark goes on to describe the consequences: "And immediately they left their nets and followed him" (Mk 1:18). Following Christ means quite literally: walking with Jesus, setting out on a journey, leaving everything, sharing his life as a poor, homeless wanderer. The circle of people who walk with Jesus soon becomes bigger. A rather large group develops that shares with him his life as a poor itinerant preacher. Out of this growing circle, he selects twelve men at a specific moment. Mark writes: Jesus "went up on a mountain, and called to him those whom he himself wanted; and they came to him. And he created (*epoiesen*) twelve, to be with him, that he might send them out to preach and to have authority to cast out demons" (Mk 3:13–15, according to the translation of Gerhard Lohfink). A list of the twelve apostles then follows.

What role does this circle of the Twelve play? Are they, so to speak, the original model for discipleship? Does everyone who wants to follow Jesus have to fit into this pattern, or does everyone have a particular commission? Are they a core group that as many as possible are then supposed to join? Or are they a special group that stands only for itself? As is so often the case, there is no either-or here but, rather, a both-and. The Church, as we profess her in the Creed, is apolitical. The Twelve are no doubt the core of the apostolic ministry. Jesus deliberately chose them in order to give his community, his family, a clear structure. Mark says that he "created" the Twelve. The expression is the same as the one used on the first page of the Bible for the creation of the world. Jesus performs an act of creation, a new creation. God creates them, as he creates the world. He creates the world out of nothing, and the calling of the Twelve also is something entirely new. The Bible uses this expression earlier for the People Israel; God creates the Chosen People (cf. Is 43:1). The Twelve do not think this up, but just as the Creator willed the creation of the world, so too he wills these Twelve. He calls to himself those whom he desires. He establishes them, he forms this group.

Jesus chooses the Twelve for a very particular purpose. We know from the Bible that the twelve tribes of Israel constitute the people as a whole; they are descended from the twelve sons of Jacob. The whole people of Israel, the Chosen People: Jesus intends to restore this picture. In a way it is supposed to have a new core in the twelve apostles. "You did not choose me, but I chose you", Jesus says in the Cenacle shortly before his Passion (Jn 15:16). Nor did they choose each other—they are as different

and contradictory as anyone could have imagined. There
is a tax collector Levi, Matthew, and thus a collabora-
tor with the occupying power, the Romans, and there
is a zealot, Simon the Canaanite, one of the radical enemies of the occupying power. They are now supposed
to become a community. (Compared with them, our
pastors are harmless!) In between there are people from
everyday occupations, many fishermen; we do not know
about the others.

Jesus brings these Twelve into his school of life. A large
part of the Gospels consists of showing how Jesus admitted them to his school. With incredible honesty and can-
dor, Scripture records how often they got "bad grades" or
did not do their homework, because Jesus' school of life
is not very easy. The Twelve represent the ministerial
priesthood of the Church. The college of bishops follows
the college of the twelve apostles. But the Twelve are also
something like a model group for all Christian coexistence,
for the Christian community. Jesus brought them together
in order to give them the ministerial priesthood, but also
as Mark says, so that they might "be with him". That is
the first goal of their vocation, which all Christians have
in common. To be with Jesus is the core of the Christian
vocation, the permanent basis for all Christian living. Most
of what we know about Jesus' "school of life" we know
from what Jesus did with his twelve apostles and how they
learned from him. It is striking that Jesus chose no "specialists" for this purpose, which is a major challenge to the
Church today. There is not one single scribe, no Pharisee,
no one from the group of those who were particularly
involved in religion, and no Sadducee, either, from the
religious priestly elite of the Temple in Jerusalem. They

are all simple "laymen". It is the Church's faith that Jesus made them priests, shepherds, by giving them the order: "Do this in remembrance of me" (Lk 22:19).

The Acts of the Apostles say this explicitly. When Peter and John stand before the council, because they healed a lame man at the Beautiful Gate of the Temple, they are examined as to why they did that and, above all, why they are propagating the name of Jesus. After that, it says in the Acts of the Apostles: "Now when they saw the boldness of Peter and John, and perceived that they were uneducated, common men, they wondered; and they recognized that they had been with Jesus" (Acts 4:13). In the Greek text we find here the word *idiotai* (from which our word "idiot" comes). This means that Jesus selects uneducated persons as witnesses to his Good News. The rulers at the council "recognized that they had been with Jesus". I wish that people could also recognize that we were with Jesus! As important as it may be to study theology, the crucial thing is to be with Jesus. That is how these simple men have the wisdom and the courage to profess Jesus before the council and to bear witness to him.

Jesus' Family

In Jesus' school, the Twelve must become new men. For this purpose, Jesus wants to make them his family. They have to learn a new kind of togetherness, the most profound basis and real secret of which is none other than the togetherness of Jesus with the Father. Later in the Cenacle, Jesus would pray for his Twelve and for all who would one day come to the faith through them, "that they may all be one; even as you, Father, are in me, and I in you ... that they may be one even as we are one" (Jn 17:21–22). From Jesus they are supposed to learn how to be one with the Father and what it means to be Jesus' family.

In Israel there were various models of how one could be a disciple. The teacher-pupil relationship plays a major role in Judaism. One goes to a rabbi to become his pupil so as to study the Torah. It is wonderful how in Jewish life even today this teacher-pupil relationship between a rabbi and his pupils is lived out. Paul himself was the pupil of Gamaliel; he recalls that he sat at the feet of that great rabbi and learned from him (cf. Acts 22:3). The rabbis have their circles of pupils. In a rabbi's circle of pupils, the Torah, God's Law, is at the center. Everything revolves around it. At Yeshiva University in New York, I witnessed young students who with incredible enthusiasm study the Torah and its interpretation by the Mishnah and the Talmud. I can only marvel at that, and I wish that we would study, work through, and indeed "chew on" Sacred Scripture with the same enthusiasm.

With Jesus and his pupils, of course, it is different. Rainer Riesner, a great German Lutheran exegete, put it this way: "Jesus' disciples are fundamentally different from rabbinic students, above all in that Jesus bound his disciples to his own person."[7] He is the center of this circle of disciples. They are supposed to learn of him. He is the living Torah. In the Sermon on the Mount, when he says: "You have heard that it was said ..." (namely, in the Torah and its interpretation), "but I say to you", he is the center. No

[7] Rainer Riesner, *Jesus als Lehrer* (Tübingen, 1981), 417; cf. Martin Hengel, *The Charismatic Leader and His Followers*, trans. James Greig (New York: Crossroad, 1981).

rabbi would have dared to put himself in the center as Jesus
did. Is that a case of overestimating himself? A sort of guru
mentality? Or is it because he really is the Master? "You
call me Teacher [Master] and Lord; and you are right, for
so I am", Jesus says (Jn 13:13–14). But he says that in the
Cenacle during the Last Supper when he has just washed
the feet of the apostles. That is the chore of a servant, the
lowliest imaginable. The disciples do not come to him
to study the Torah, to discuss it with one another, and to
interpret it; instead, he himself is the Law in person. On
the mount of the Beatitudes, he gives the disciples the new
Law, as God gave Moses the Torah on Mount Sinai. Now
if Jesus himself is the center of his circle of disciples, then
that also changes the network of relationships among the
people who have him at their center.

The teacher-pupil relationship changes in communion
with Jesus. But family ties also change in Jesus' milieu.
Jesus' own family first has to experience that bitterly. Mark
records that Jesus' relatives come to Capernaum to take
him back home to Nazareth, back to their family, because
they say he has gone mad (cf. Mk 3:21). They want to take
him back forcibly. There is a family egotism, a clannish
mentality, which is incompatible with following Jesus.
The family of Jesus tries to do it again, this time somewhat more carefully. The house is full of people, Jesus is
inside, and many people are with him. Then someone tells
him: "Your mother and your brethren are outside, asking for you" (Mk 3:32). One would expect Jesus to stand
up immediately and to go outside and greet his family.
His reaction is quite different: "Who are my mother and
my brethren?" Then he points to the people around him
and says: "Whoever does the will of God is my brother,

and sister, and mother." Not blood ties or family pride, but a new family. Following Jesus is something different from a work contract, a partnership, or a "joint mission", so to speak, in which people collaborate for a while and then go their separate ways. Following Jesus results in a new tie, a new fellowship; one becomes a member of Jesus' family. We become his siblings, indeed, his mother. At the same time, however, those who are admitted to his family must be willing to separate themselves from their natural family, if necessary through conflict, with divisions and enmity. "Thus Jesus required of his disciples a deter-mined turning away from their own families.... Common life with Jesus took the place of family.... The disciples' community of life with Jesus was a *community of destiny*. It went so far that the disciples had to be prepared to suffer what Jesus suffered—if necessary, even persecution or exe-cution" (Gerhard Lohfink).[8] The most beautiful thing that can happen is when your own family grows to be a part of Jesus' family. This can often be a painful process that occurs only by way of repentance and conversion, in which fleshly, natural family ties become something new through faith. Christ transforms them: in friendship, in relation to his own family, he turns them into what God made them to be. This then gives rise to the deep security that Jesus' family should give us, despite all the uncertainty of the journey of discipleship. When Jesus says: "You have one teacher, and you are all brethren" (Mt 23:8), it shows then this new relationship that is supposed to develop between us as we follow him.

---

[8] Gerhard Lohfink, *Jesus and Community*, trans. John P. Galvin (Philadelphia: Fortress Press, 1984), 33; cf. Friedrich Bechina, "Die Kirche als 'Familie Gottes'", *Analecta Gregoriana* 272 (1998): 349.

Is Everyone Called to Discipleship?

Are we all called to discipleship? Is being a Christian the same as discipleship? The answer is not all that simple. In the New Testament we find passages where it very clearly says: We are all called to discipleship. Thus Saint Paul says in the First Letter to the Corinthians: "God is faithful, by whom you were called into the fellowship of his Son, Jesus Christ our Lord" (1 Cor 1:9). Or: "Only, let every one lead the life which the Lord has assigned to him, and in which God has called him" (1 Cor 7:17). Therefore, everybody has a call to fellowship with Christ, but the call can take very different forms. In the discourse on the bread of heaven in the synagogue of Capernaum, Jesus says, citing Isaiah 54:13: "And they shall all be taught by God" (Jn 6:45).

We are all called to go to Jesus' school. We are all called to holiness. That is the core teaching of Vatican II. The central fifth chapter of the Constitution on the Church, *Lumen gentium*, deals with "The Universal Call to Holiness in the Church". "You, therefore, must be perfect, as your heavenly Father is perfect" (Mt 5:48).

The Council says: "Thus it is evident to everyone that all the faithful of Christ, of whatever rank or status, are called to the fullness of the Christian life and to the perfection of charity" (*Lumen gentium* 40). When a pope is declared a saint, it is not because he was pope but, rather, because he lived out his Christian life in an exemplary way. In this he has no advantage over any other Christian. The way to holiness is open to everyone, but the vocations, the paths of holiness, are different, depending on the calling that each one has received.

Are all called to be disciples of Jesus? The question has stirred up debate through all the centuries. Was Jesus' radical call directed to everyone or only to a few with a special calling? To whom do the words of Jesus apply: "The harvest is plentiful, but the laborers are few; pray therefore the Lord of the harvest to send out laborers into his harvest" (Mt 9:37–38)? We like to quote these words in intercessions for vocations to the priesthood and the religious life. That is not unwarranted, but it is not the whole story. Surely there is one correct intuition here: to be sent into the Lord's harvest is a special calling, for which we should pray to the Lord. Not everyone is sent to do this task. Jesus' saying presupposes that there are others who are not called to do that but should still pray that the Lord will send enough laborers into his harvest.

The Gospels show us that "Jesus does not call everyone to follow him."[9] He does call everyone to conversion: "Repent, and believe in the gospel" (Mk 1:15), but he does not call everyone to follow him directly. He calls the tax collector Levi-Matthew away from his tax office: "Follow me" (Mk 2:14). To Zacchaeus, another tax collector in Jericho, Jesus directs no call to follow him. He remains at his job. But he has converted. His life has become new, while his occupation remains the same (cf. Lk 19:1–10). We find this difference in the women, too. Luke reports:

Soon afterward [Jesus] went on through cities and villages, preaching and bringing the good news of the kingdom of God. And the Twelve were with him, and also some women who had been healed of evil spirits and infirmities:

---

[9] Gerhard Lohfink, *Wie hat Jesus Gemeinde gewollt?* 2nd, expanded ed. (Freiburg im Breisgau, 1993), 206.

Mary, called Magdalene, from whom seven demons had
gone out, and Joanna, the wife of Chuza, Herod's steward,
and Susanna, and many others, who provided for them out
of their means. (Lk 8:1–3)

The women traveled with Jesus from Galilee to Jerusalem,
conduct which at that time was certainly rather unusual.
They did not run away when Jesus was crucified. "All
his acquaintances and the women who had followed him
from Galilee stood at a distance and saw these things"
(Lk 23:49). Those women were present at his burial and
came to the tomb early in the morning two days later
with the spices and ointments that they had prepared
(cf. Lk 23:55—24:1).

Are these women in some special way "female disciples"? In any case, there are others who are quite close to
Jesus, indeed, are friends with him, but do not follow him
on his journey and have no special mission. I am thinking here of Jesus' beloved friends in Bethany, Martha,
Mary, and Lazarus, in whose house Jesus knew that he was
always welcome.

From this Gerhard Lohfink concludes: "Jesus does not
call all of Israel to discipleship. Besides the disciples there is
a broad spectrum of people who are open to the gospel of
Jesus and take seriously his call to conversion but do not
follow him directly. And so automatically there are three
groups: the circle of the Twelve, which in the Gospels is
already identified with 'the apostles'; the circle of disciples that is considerably larger but likewise follows Jesus
directly; and finally the people, insofar as they accept
Jesus' message positively."[10]

[10] Ibid., 209.

Apostles—disciples—people. Is this not once again a distinction that leads to "stratification"? There is a danger of seeing "those with vocations" here and "the people" there and discriminating between those who spend their lives following Christ and those who remain in the world. Is not the common vocation of all Christians, of all the baptized, lost in the process? This danger always existed, and it still exists today. It disappears, however, as soon as we look at the core of Jesus' message. Not all are called to the same way of life in following Christ, but all are called to conversion. The Sermon on the Mount, with its truly radical words, is true for all, whether they are "settled" or "itinerant" Christians, "disciples" or "people". The Sermon on the Mount demands that we refrain not only from a wicked deed but also from every angry word against our brethren in faith (Mt 5:22). It requires us "to take the marriage of another person (and of course one's own as well) so seriously that one does not even look with desire at another woman" (cf. Mt 5:29–30). It demands "an end to the disguising and twisting of language, so that only unequivocal meaning remains" (cf. Mt 5:37) and "that we give to everyone who asks us for something" (cf. Mt 5:42).[11]

This applies to all Christians. Here there is no two-tiered ethics, a more perfect way of life of the apostles and disciples and a less perfect way for the rest of the People of God. The two ways of life are mutually complementary. That was already the case in the early Church, and it is no different today: the disciples who are on the road need the "houses" that open their doors to them, the families

[11] Ibid., 212.

who welcome and support them. But both ways of life are about "total self-giving": it consists of doing God's will in everyday life. The universal call to holiness lies always in loving "more", in ever greater dedication.

Jesus likes to illustrate this "more" with people who are not even acquainted with him. The most moving example of this is when Jesus points out to his disciples the poor widow in the Temple, who is completely unaware of what is happening. She threw only two small copper coins into the Temple treasury, much less than the others. But they all merely gave something out of their abundance. She, in contrast, gave everything that she had to live on, literally: "her whole living". Therefore, Jesus says, she gave "*more* than all those" (Mk 12:41–44).

Does being a Christian mean being a disciple of Jesus? That was our question at the outset. If by that you mean following Jesus on the road as the apostles and the male and female disciples did, then not all who believe in Christ are also called to this way of life. But all are called to conversion and to the radical demands of the Sermon on the Mount. Jesus himself is the master teacher of this way. Looking at him and living in communion with him is the universal school of life for all who believe in him.

Let those, however, to whom the gift and grace of faith has been granted recall the Gospel for Christ the King Sunday: At the Last Judgment, the just did not realize at all that they had encountered Christ and served God, nor did the damned. They simply saw their neighbor in need or else overlooked him; they helped or neglected to help (cf. Mt 25:31–46). We are all invited to Jesus' school of life. One of the most important lessons in this school, which never closes, is to see with astonishment and gratitude that others in that school are much farther along than we are. Sometimes these are even those who are entirely unaware that they are in this school of life and do not know how successful they have been at learning.

III

"Lord, Teach Us to Pray"

Jesus' School of Prayer

In Jesus' school of life, everyone is cordially welcome. But as in every school, you also have to want to learn. So I ask myself: What do I want to learn from Jesus? Someone who goes to a violin teacher wants to learn how to play the violin. Someone who goes to driving school wants to learn to drive. But what do I want to learn in Jesus' school? Do I personally know an answer to this simple question?

Getting to Know Jesus

The first two men who followed Jesus were disciples of John the Baptist: Andrew, the brother of Simon Peter, and the beloved disciple (John, as tradition has assumed with good reasons). As they walked behind Jesus, he turned around and asked, "What do you seek?" (Jn 1:38). What do we want? What are we seeking? What do I hope to learn from Jesus? Do I hope anything at all? The question is worthwhile. It may also lead to a painful surprise: Have I given any thought whatsoever to what I want to learn from Jesus?

In the field of education, they like to talk about "learning goals". What is my learning goal? Am I willing to learn, eager to learn something from Jesus? When Jesus asked, "What do you seek?" the two future disciples answered: "Teacher, where are you staying?" Usually it begins with wanting to get acquainted with someone. Do we know Jesus?[1] "Come and see", was Jesus' answer. The first learning goal of the apostles was to get to know Jesus. The passage goes on to say: "They came and saw where he was staying; and they stayed with him that day" (Jn 1:39). That is the first and most important thing in Jesus' school of life: getting to know him personally. The teachings of Jesus are important, but first we need to converse with him, to become familiar with him, to establish a friendship with him. Jesus' school of life is not primarily about acquiring as much knowledge as possible, even though that is important. It is not about something but about someone. Knowing him and loving him are the greatest learning achievement. "We wish to see Jesus" (Jn 12:21), said the Greeks—pagans who had come to Jerusalem for the Passover—to the disciples of Jesus: here again, curiosity, the desire to get to know this man, interest in the one about whom people were saying so much. Without interest, there is no learning. Everyone who studies or works in the field of education knows that.

A second question is just as important: What does Jesus want to teach us? What is his pedagogical goal? We go to school because we want or have to learn. But the teachers determine what we learn. What does Jesus intend to teach us?

[1] Cf. Hans Urs von Balthasar, *Does Jesus Know Us—Do We Know Him?* trans. Graham Harrison (San Francisco: Ignatius Press, 1983).

There is an expression that occurs so often in Jesus' teaching that we get the impression that it is the epitome of what Jesus wanted to teach: the phrase "kingdom of God" or, in the Gospel of Matthew (in order to avoid saying God's name), "kingdom of heaven". Right at the beginning of Mark's Gospel, we read: "Now after John was arrested, Jesus came into Galilee, preaching the gospel of God, and saying, 'The time is fulfilled, and the kingdom of God is at hand; repent, and believe in the gospel'" (Mk 1:14–15). Matthew talks about "the gospel of the kingdom" (Mt 4:23). But what is Jesus trying to teach when he speaks about the "kingdom of God" or about the "kingdom of heaven"? In the Synoptic Gospels alone, that is, in Matthew, Mark, and Luke, the expression "kingdom of God" occurs ninety-nine times, ninety of them on Jesus' lips. In all, it occurs 122 times in the New Testament. Jesus' teaching clearly emphasizes the kingdom of God. It is Jesus' message.[2]

Jesus announces that the kingdom of God is coming, it is near; it is burgeoning, growing, and being opposed. But what is the kingdom of God, and what are we supposed to learn about it? Jesus says on one occasion that we should be "trained for the kingdom of heaven", for the kingdom of God (Mt 13:52). We should become pupils, learners, and since learning is not an end in itself, we should also be capable of becoming teachers of the kingdom of God.

Jesus' disciples learned initially, not through Jesus' words, but through his deeds and even more from himself. His example, his conduct, was the first school. Even before it was a question of doctrine, it was about his person. What really remains in our memory is what a person represents.

[2] Cf. Joseph Ratzinger/Benedict XVI, *Jesus of Nazareth*, vol. 1, trans. Adrian J. Walker (New York: Doubleday, 2007), 62.

When I remember my wonderful German teacher in secondary school, it is above all the impression of his personality that has stayed with me. The poems that we had to learn by heart I have forgotten to a great extent.

Jesus' Prayer

One feature in Jesus' life impressed and influenced the disciples and probably has a lot to tell us about Jesus' teaching and even more about his person: namely, Jesus' prayer. Mark describes Jesus' first day in Capernaum, his public ministry after he moved from Nazareth to Capernaum. It was a day of intense encounters, with a healing in the synagogue. On the evening of the Sabbath, when the Sabbath rest was over, the people came in droves to his house. He healed many sick and possessed people. A successful, very intense first day. Then, though, on the next day (this is after the Sabbath and therefore the first day of the week), we read in Mark: "In the morning, a great while before day, he rose and went out to a lonely place, and there he prayed" (Mk 1:35).

The disciples look for him and find him. They are surprised. What are you doing here? What is this? They are freshmen, after all, just beginning in Jesus' school of life. Certainly they were impressed by what they had experienced, by the first healings and exorcisms. But what unmistakably impressed them and probably led them most deeply to discipleship was the experience that their teacher prayed for hours, all night long. He used to withdraw to a solitary place, often to a mountain, to pray. The disciples "caught" him at it. Without wasting many words of his own about it, through his prayer he probably elicited a profound longing for discipleship. Through the experience of him praying, through his example, he awakens the yearning of the disciples to do the same.

What is going on in his mind and heart when he spends so much time in prayer? Prayer is fascinating. The first confreres of Saint Dominic (d. 1221), the Father of our Order, liked to watch him as he prayed alone in church at night. In the Basilica of Santa Sabina in Rome on the Aventine Hill, there is to this day a little window through which you can look down into the church, and tradition says that there the brothers used to watch how he prayed for hours at night. It must have been similar with the first disciples of Jesus. Luke tells us: "[Jesus] was praying in a certain place, and when he ceased, one of his disciples said to him, 'Lord, teach us to pray, as John taught his disciples'" (Lk 11:1). Then Jesus teaches them the Our Father. The impressive thing about this scene is the note of respect that we sense. They do not dare to interrupt Jesus as he prays. They wait until he has ended his prayer. How long did it last?

When Pope John Paul II (d. 2005), during his third pastoral visit to Austria in 1998, entered the cathedral in Salzburg for the liturgy, a short time of prayer was scheduled before the tabernacle at a side altar. Obviously he had completely forgotten that thousands of people and the television cameras were waiting, and he spent twenty minutes praying there. I will never forget how immersed he was in prayer. A human being's prayer automatically elicits respect and carefulness, at least in people who are to some degree sensitive to it.

This is the mystery of prayer. Prayer is universal, just as universal as religion. It is simply part of being human.

Therefore, it also makes sense and is possible to write a phenomenology of prayer, a description of the attitude of prayer, of various methods and forms of prayer. Friedrich Heiler (d. 1967) wrote a thick book entitled: *Prayer: A Study in the History and Psychology of Religion* [trans. Samuel McComb (London and New York: Oxford Univ. Press, 1932)]. In it he described comparatively, without value judgments, how people pray.

For me it was unforgettable to witness women praying in a Buddhist temple in Taiwan in 1977. Prayer is unmistakable, impressive, for instance, if you come into a mosque where men have prostrated themselves to pray. Learning to pray is part of the journey of religious life in all religions. You have to learn formulas and forms. Prayers have their traditions. I was very impressed to receive in Turkey a booklet for young Muslims about the types of prayer, the expressive forms of praying, the physical postures, and so on. That is a school of prayer. Normally one learns prayer at home, from parents or grandparents. How many people in the Soviet Union still learned to pray from their *babushka*, their grandmother. In this way, Jesus too probably learned to pray from his parents and in the synagogue in the tradition of his people. The Jewish world of prayer is fascinating, a great treasure of the culture of prayer, with its psalms and liturgical prayers. "[Jesus] learns to pray in the words and rhythms of the prayer of his people, in the synagogue at Nazareth and the Temple at Jerusalem", we read in the *Catechism* (*CCC* 2599). There is something special about the Jewish world of prayer in comparison to other religions. It has a familiarity with God that is something new. Jewish prayer is a response to a God who addresses man and reveals himself to him. This can lead to an intimacy and a closeness that is foreign to other religions. It is no accident that the Jewish people, the Chosen People, is addressed by God's prophet with the utmost familiarity as "my son" (cf. Hos 11:1; Mt 2:15). But what the disciples experience with Jesus goes much farther. This is unique even in Judaism, a degree of familiarity that we do not find in the great Jewish tradition. Very early on Jesus makes us sense that there is one thing about his life that is unparalleled. When the twelve-year-old Jesus remains in the Temple in Jerusalem, his worried parents look for him. "After three days, they found him in the temple, sitting among the teachers, listening to them and asking them questions." Mary says: "Your father and I have been looking for you anxiously." Jesus seems to be surprised at that. "How is it that you sought me? Did you not know that I must be in my Father's house?" Jesus says literally: "I must be occupied with the things that pertain to my Father" (Lk 2:46, 48–49). Something new is revealed here that is scarcely comprehensible for his parents. The intimacy that Jesus has with God, whom he calls his Father, is something unparalleled.

Prayer to the Triune God

Many say that the Church made Jesus, the simple man from Galilee in Nazareth, into God. She deified him and exalted him to the status of Son of God. Apart from the discussion within Christendom, this question has acquired great relevance today because of Islam. For if there is one point at which Islam criticizes Christianity fundamentally, it is the claim about Jesus' divinity. From the beginning it was the central objection that Islam leveled at Christianity. Of course, at the beginning of his career, Muhammad fought against the "older Arab polytheism", but experts say his attack against the belief in the triune God became increasingly pronounced, the accusation that Christians believed in three gods and were therefore ultimately polytheists.[3]

The famous Surah 112 in the Qur'an reads: "Say: He is Allah, the One and Only; Allah, the Eternal, Absolute; He begetteth not, nor is He begotten; And there is none like unto Him." (This Surah, incidentally, is inscribed on the Dome of the Rock in Jerusalem.) This seems, then, to be aimed expressly against the Christian profession of faith, because the Christian Creed says that Christ is the Son of God, "begotten, not made". The Qur'an understands that quite radically, as we see in Surah 4:48, where belief in many gods is described as an unforgivable sin. It reads: "Indeed, Allah does not forgive association [of other gods] with Him, but He forgives what is less than that for whom He wills. And he who associates others [that is, other gods] with Allah has certainly fabricated a tremendous sin." This seems to mean that all other sins can be forgiven, but this sin of associating other gods with Allah cannot be forgiven.[4]

Do Christians pray to three gods? Is our Christian prayer idolatry? We pray to the Father in the Our Father, then again we pray to Jesus, for instance, in the Jesus Prayer or in the individual prayers of the liturgy, or we pray to the Holy Spirit: *Veni creator spiritus* ("Come, Holy Ghost, Creator blest"). Are we praying then always to the same

[3] Cf. Gerhard Lohfink, *Beten schenkt Heimat: Theologie und Praxis des christlichen Gebets* (Freiburg im Breisgau, 2010), 30.

[4] Cf. ibid., 30–31.

God, to one God? That is a vital question. Can we give
an account of our faith? Are we able to give arguments for
why we believe in the one God—Father, Son, and Holy
Spirit, one God in three Persons? We must become still
more capable of proclaiming our faith, but it is not enough
just to have reasonable arguments. The decisive question is
the existential one: How do we pray? Do we pray to three
gods? Or do we pray to the one God when we pray to the
Father, to the Son, and to the Holy Spirit?

We have to go to Jesus' school and ask: How did you
pray, Lord? Show us what your prayer is like. What is his
prayer about, if Jesus is the Son of God? Does God pray
to God? What does it mean that Jesus prayed for hours at
night? Precisely through their experience of Jesus' prayer,
the disciples seem to have found the most profound access
to the mystery of Jesus. Indeed, just when they see Jesus
praying and experience him at prayer, the innermost mystery of Jesus is revealed to them.

Here I would like, so to speak, to take the hand of my
teacher Joseph Ratzinger/Benedict XVI, who in an especially incisive and impressive essay from the early 1980s,
entitled "Taking Bearings in Christology",[5] tried to start
from Jesus' prayer and sense the innermost mystery of
Jesus, just as the apostles did when they saw Jesus pray. It is
a matter of getting a glimpse of the place where Jesus lives,
where he has his center, where his heart is, his source. This
center is the word "Abba", dear Father. When Jesus prays,
he is with his Abba, with the Father. And so the disciples
experience it. Certainly everyone who prays is directed

[5] Joseph Ratzinger, "Taking Bearings in Christology", in *Behold the Pierced One*
(San Francisco: Ignatius Press, 1986), 13–46.

somehow toward God. But when Jesus is with God in his prayer, he is so like no one else. What the disciples sensed on that occasion awoke in them the yearning to get to know this place: "Teacher, where are you staying?— Come and see" (Jn 1:38–39). Again and again this moves me. This encounter of the first two disciples with Jesus is something like a key: "Teacher, where are you staying?" Not only: What is your address, but: Where are you at home, where is the secret of your life, your abode (*pou meneis*)? It is purely and simply the word Abba. Jesus is, as John says in the prologue, "with the Father", or even more explicitly at the conclusion thereof: "in the bosom of the Father" (Jn 1:1, 18).

The disciples surely did not arrive at such a clear insight right at the start, when in the early morning they set out from Capernaum, looked for Jesus, and then found him somewhere in nature, as he was praying in solitude. They experience Jesus in a unique dialogue. By conversing with him, they understand more and more that his words and his deeds, his whole being, come from this source. They sense that Jesus does not speak on his own, does not act on his own, but rather that his life comes from this dialogue with the Father. "For the entire gospel testimony is unanimous that Jesus' words and deeds flowed from his most intimate communion with the Father."[6] That is the source. Before Jesus selected the Twelve from the first group of his disciples, Luke tells us, he spent the whole night praying on a mountain. Joseph Ratzinger comments: "The calling of the Twelve proceeds from prayer, from the Son's converse with the Father. The Church is born in that prayer

[6] Ibid., 17.

in which Jesus gives himself back into the Father's hands and the Father commits everything to the Son. This most profound communication of Son and Father conceals the Church's true and ever-new origin, which is also her firm foundation (Lk 6:12–17)."[7] Jesus draws from this constant inner union with his Abba, the Father.

Cardinal Ratzinger mentions a second example, in which Luke again reminds us that Jesus was at prayer. It is the moment near Caesarea Philippi, when Peter acknowledges Jesus as the Messiah, the Christ. In Luke we read: "Now it happened that as [Jesus] was praying alone the disciples were with him; and he asked them, 'Who do the people say that I am?' ... And he said to them, 'But who do you say that I am?'" Whereupon Peter professes that he is the Messiah (Lk 9:18–20). "In this way the Evangelist makes it clear that Peter had grasped and expressed the most fundamental reality of the person of Jesus as a result of having seen him praying, in fellowship with the Father.... We see who Jesus is if we see him at prayer." When we Christians profess Jesus as Messiah and Son of God, that is not a theory, not a hypothesis, but rather something that is revealed in prayer. Once again Cardinal Ratzinger: "The whole of Christology—our speaking of Christ—is nothing other than the interpretation of his prayer."[8] Jesus is one with the Father; the disciples learned this when they experienced him praying. Thus the fundamental Christian profession, that he is the Son, comes more from experience than from Jesus' words. "You are the Christ, the Son of the living God", says Peter. Jesus says: "Flesh and blood has not revealed this to you, but my Father who is

[7] Ibid., 18.
[8] Ibid., 19, 20.

in heaven" (Mt 16:16–17). To acknowledge this is not a matter of theory but, rather, a matter of revelation, which is conveyed by way of the heart. "The entire person of Jesus is contained in his prayer."[9]

How does Jesus allow his prayer to emerge when he expresses it in speech? After all, most of the time he prays in silence, in the night on the mountain, in solitude. The Gospel records for us as one example of a prayer Jesus' "jubilation" or shout of joy after the severe disappointment about the unbelief in the places where he is ministering, Chorazin, Bethsaida, and Capernaum (cf. Mt 11:20–24):

> I thank you, Father, Lord of heaven and earth, that you have hidden these things from the wise and understanding and revealed them to infants; yes, Father, for such was your gracious will. All things have been delivered to me by my Father; and no one knows the Son except the Father, and no one knows the Father except the Son and any one to whom the Son chooses to reveal him. (Mt 11:25–27)

Father and Son are different and yet so completely one that we cannot honor and adore the Father without the Son or the Son without the Father. This is the answer to the challenge from Islam: When we pray to Christ, we are not praying to another god. Then this is not someone "whom we associate with God", as the Qur'an says. That would be a misunderstanding of Christian prayer, to which Christians themselves perhaps have contributed. Rather, we pray through Jesus Christ to the Father in the Holy Spirit. We never pray to the Father without the Son. We never pray to the Holy Spirit without the Father and the Son. Jesus is

[9] Ibid., 20.

one with the Father, "consubstantial (one in being) with the Father". Maybe that is expressed most forcefully in the few words of prayer on the Cross that tradition has handed down to us. Precisely in this extreme situation of deadly peril, Jesus prays. All four Gospels present Jesus during his Passion to us as someone who prays. According to the Gospels, Cardinal Ratzinger says, "Jesus died praying. He fashioned his death into an act of prayer, an act of worship."[10] First: "Father, forgive them; for they know not what they do" (Lk 23:34). "My God, my God, why have you forsaken me?" from Psalm 22:2 (Mk 15:34). Then he prays to the Father before the loud cry with which he dies: "Father, into your hands I commit my spirit" (Lk 23:46). To his last breath, until he breathes out his Spirit on the Cross, Jesus is wholly prayer. His living and his dying are completely one with the Father.

The Spirit Prays in Us

"Lord, teach us to pray." When I look at Jesus, at how he prays, and see that his whole life is prayer, then I am tempted to say: I cannot learn that. I will never manage to do that, it is completely beyond my capabilities. I do pray at many moments of the day. But how are we frail human beings, who can scarcely perform a consistent act of the will, who can scarcely pray one Our Father while concentrating, supposed to be as immersed in prayer as Jesus is, who does not pray alongside other things, but whose very essence and life are prayer? Surely we know of

[10] Ibid., 22.

people who are rocks of prayer. One is Pope John Paul II. Another impressive example is Padre Pio (d. 1968). Nevertheless, such a great master of prayer as Paul says: "We do not know how to pray as we ought" (Rom 8:26). For this reason he comes to the conclusion: Only God can do it! God himself must pray in us, otherwise nothing will come of it. "The Spirit himself intercedes for us with sighs too deep for words. And he who searches the hearts of men knows what is the mind of the Spirit, because the Spirit intercedes for the saints according to the will of God" (Rom 8:26–27).[11]

We are still infinitely far away from the prayer that lives in the Heart of Jesus, from this exchange between the Father and the Son that encompasses his whole life. We see Jesus pray, we want to pray as he does and sigh over our inability. Not only do we not know what we really ought to pray for; we do not know, either, *how* we really ought to pray. The painful sigh of our inability: the more we sense how far short we fall of Jesus' prayer, this perfect Being-in-God, this conversation within the Divinity, the more willing we are to go to school with Jesus in earnest. As a teacher he is different from our school instructors, professors, and catechists, for he can teach through the Spirit, for whom we can only beg. The Holy Spirit teaches us to pray; indeed, he himself prays in us. "You are not the one who prays. Prayer is not a work of the human mind. The smaller our share in it, the better we pray", says a spiritual master from the seventeenth century (Claude Séguenot, d. 1676). With empty hands we go to Jesus' "School of Prayer". He, the true Master of prayer,

---

[11] Cf. Lohfink, *Beten schenkt Heimat*, 25.

makes us his children, his sons and daughters. Through his Spirit he himself prays in us. That is the real secret of Christian prayer. However poor our prayer may be, the Holy Spirit who prays in us makes it possible for us really to be able to pray ourselves after all, simply and confidently, like children who are able to speak to their father.

Gerhard Lohfink writes: "Praying ultimately means settling into the conversation between the Father, the Son, and the Holy Spirit, not by our own power and ability, but empowered by the status of Child that is granted to the Christian in baptism."[12] In this power we can dare to be praying pupils in Jesus' school.

---

[12] Ibid., 28.

IV

"But I Say to You . . ."

The Sermon on the Mount as Jesus' School of Life

It was in the year 391, when an already renowned rhetor, Augustine (d. 430), was visiting Hippo, a seaport in North Africa. Bishop Valerius was old and ailing and wanted a helper, a priest who would assist him. When he heard that the famous Augustine was in the church, he decided then and there to lay hands on him. The people were enthusiastic and pushed Augustine toward the front. He had no chance to escape this enthusiasm. So he was suddenly a priest and was supposed to help the ailing bishop by taking over his preaching duties.

We do not have priestly ordinations like that any more. In the ancient Church, it was not unusual at all for hands to be imposed on someone on the spot when the people urgently wanted him as a priest.

Augustine noticed that he was inadequately prepared for his new duty, and he asked his bishop for a few months' time in which to prepare. He writes in a letter: [Ep. 21, 3]

> Now that I know my illness, I ought to examine carefully all the remedies of [the Lord's] scriptures and, by praying and reading, work that he may grant my soul health suited

for such dangerous tasks. I did not do this before because
I did not have the time.... I learned through actual experience what a man needs who ministers to the people the
sacrament and word of God.... [May I not be] permitted
to pursue what I have learned that I lack?[1]

Augustine therefore withdrew and used the time to study
Sacred Scripture intensively. In those days, that meant
learning them largely by heart. Until the modern era, it
was not at all uncommon for individuals to know Sacred
Scripture mostly by heart, just as today there are still many
people who know the Qur'an by heart, even children,
who are very proudly displayed. Christianity was familiar
with this tradition, just like Judaism.

Then Augustine started his preaching ministry and
gave his first series of sermons about the Sermon on the
Mount.[2] "Our Lord Jesus Christ gave this sermon on a
mountain, as we read in Matthew's Gospel. Anyone who
reads it reverently and soberly will find in it, I believe, the
perfect manner of Christian living (*perfectum vitae christianae
modum*), with regard to what pertains to the best morals (*ad
mores optimos pertinet*)" (I, 1). In the Sermon on the Mount,
therefore, we learn the perfect Christian life.

Obviously Augustine thought that it was not asking
too much of his very simple parishioners in that seaport to
meditate on the Sermon on the Mount. "For Augustine

---

[1] Augustine, Ep. 21, 3, in: *The Works of Saint Augustine: A Translation for the 21st
Century*, vol. 2/1, *Letters 1–99*, trans. Roland Teske, S.J. (Hyde Park, N.Y.: New
City Press, 2001), 56.

[2] The original German edition cites here an abridged German translation of
Augustine's series of homilies on the Sermon of the Mount. The author goes on,
however, to translate quotations directly from the Latin. In each case the English
text is a literal rendering of the author's German version of the quotation.—TRANS.

and the early Church, the Sermon on the Mount is directed to the whole people and thus to all Christians" (Susanne Greiner).[3] Is that really the case? Is the Sermon on the Mount *the* Magna Carta of Christian living and thus the charter for Jesus' school of life? Does it show the way in which discipleship is to be lived out? Augustine is convinced that nowhere is the foundation of Christian living shown so clearly as in the Sermon on the Mount. Augustine bases his conclusion that this is precisely where the perfect manner of Christian living is presented on the words of Jesus with which the Sermon on the Mount ends:

> Every one then who hears these words of mine and does them will be like a wise man who built his house upon the rock; and the rain fell, and the floods came, and the winds blew and beat upon that house, but it did not fall, because it had been founded on the rock. (Mt 7:24–25)

Jesus says quite specifically: "*these* words *of mine*". For Augustine, the rock foundation on which the house of Christian living can be built solidly is found in the words of the Sermon on the Mount and in obeying them. He says in his first sermon: "These words spoken on the mountain should so completely configure the lives of all who try to obey them that they can rightly be compared to someone who builds on rock" (I, 1). The Sermon on the Mount is therefore the charter of Christian living.

Can we measure somewhat by our obedience to the Sermon on the Mount how far we have progressed in Jesus' school of discipleship? Is the Sermon on the Mount

[3] Aurelius Augustinus, *Die Bergpredigt*, selections translated into German by Susanne Greiner, Christliche Meister 54 (Freiburg im Breisgau, 2006), 12n10.

the charter of Christian living, or is it the expression of an especially radical form thereof? Is Jesus' Sermon on the Mount a special morality for elite Christians, or is it addressed to all Christians, perhaps even to all mankind?

To Whom Is the Sermon on the Mount Addressed?

The Sermon on the Mount takes up three chapters in the Gospel of Matthew (5–7), beginning with the Beatitudes; then come the so-called antitheses—"You have heard it said ... but I say to you ..."—and, after that, instructions about prayer, fasting, and almsgiving (which we should perform in secret, so that only our Father in heaven sees it), and finally major instructions about trusting in God's providence: "Do not be anxious!"

To whom is the Sermon on the Mount addressed? At the beginning we read: "Seeing the crowds, [Jesus] went up on the mountain, and when he sat down his disciples came to him. And he opened his mouth and taught them" (Mt 5:1–2). Did the thousands of people not hear him; did he not speak to them? Jesus sees the many people, but he addresses his words to the disciples. Is the Sermon on the Mount instruction for disciples or instruction for the people?

Another great preacher of the early Church, Saint John Chrysostom (d. 407), writes in his homilies on the Gospel of Matthew at this passage: " 'His disciples came unto Him, and He taught them.' For that way the others also were sure to be more eagerly attentive to Him, than they would have been, had He addressed Himself unto all."[4] Maybe

---

[4] Saint John Chrysostom, *Homilies on the Gospel of Saint Matthew*, hom. 15, NPNF-1 10:91b.

for Chrysostom it was a rhetorical trick: he speaks to a few immediately surrounding him, and so the others become curious and listen all the more carefully to what he says to them. Pope Benedict elaborates on this idea:

> Jesus sits down—the expression of the plenary authority of the teacher. He takes his seat on the cathedra [the professorial chair] of the mountain.... Jesus takes his seat on the cathedra as the teacher of Israel and as the teacher of people everywhere. For ... Matthew uses the word *disciple* here not in order to restrict the intended audience of the Sermon on the Mount, but to enlarge it. Everyone who hears and accepts the word can become a "disciple."
>
> What counts from now on is hearing and following, not lineage. Discipleship is possible for everyone; it is a calling for everyone. Hearing, then, is the basis on which a more inclusive Israel is built—a renewed Israel, which does not exclude or revoke the old one, but steps beyond it into the domain of universality.[5]

All can become hearers of the Sermon on the Mount, and therefore all can become disciples.

> Both elements are true: The Sermon on the Mount is addressed to the entire world, the entire present and future, and yet it demands *discipleship* and can be understood and lived out only by following Jesus and accompanying him on his journey.[6]

The Sermon on the Mount is addressed to all people of all times, but on condition of discipleship. It begins with

[5] Joseph Ratzinger/Benedict XVI, *Jesus of Nazareth*, vol. 1, trans. Adrian J. Walker (New York: Doubleday, 2007), 65–66.
[6] Ibid., 69.

the eight Beatitudes, the inexhaustible charter of discipleship. Then come two images with which Jesus illuminates
the mission of the disciples: "You are the salt of the earth."
"You are the light of the world" (cf. Mt 5:13–14). Salt
and light apply more likely to the situation of a minority.
Normally only pinches of salt are used in food; it is not
the food itself. Light lights up the room, but it is not the
room. Here, then, is a contrast between "you" and "the
earth", "the world", between the disciples and the world.
This tension exists also in the so-called "antinomies" of
the Torah:

> "You have heard that it was said to the men of old, 'You
> shall not kill....' But I say to you that every one who
> is angry with his brother shall be liable to judgment....
> You have heard that it was said, 'You shall not commit
> adultery.' But I say to you that every one who looks at a
> woman lustfully has already committed adultery with her
> in his heart." (Mt 5:21–22, 27–28)

To whom are these antitheses directed, which make the
commandments even more radical? Do they express an
elite morality as compared to the general norm, an ideal
that is so high that it would be rather discouraging to most
people? Whom is Jesus addressing, when he says at the beginning of chapter 6: "Beware of practicing your piety
before men in order to be seen by them" (Mt 6:1)? Almsgiving, prayer, and fasting, which are the classic forms of
piety in Judaism also, should be practiced in secret, not
for show, not in order to be seen by everyone, but only
in the presence of the heavenly Father, who will also
reward them. This is followed by references to the heavenly

Father, whom we should trust: Do not be anxious, look at
the lilies of the field, the birds of the air, they neither sow
nor reap, and yet your heavenly Father feeds them (cf. Mt
6:25–26). For this reason we should pray confidently, we
should entrust ourselves to his will. This is the way that
Jesus shows in the Sermon on the Mount. Right at the
conclusion, once again: "Everyone who hears *these* words
of mine and does them ... [has] built ... upon the rock."

The Torah of the Messiah

The Sermon on the Mount consists of Jesus' words. It
is not some sort of contribution to a discussion on ethics, but the explicit statement of Jesus: "And when Jesus
finished these sayings, the crowds were astonished at his
teaching, for he taught them as one who had authority,
and not as their scribes" (Mt 7:28–29). His words cannot
be compared with academic or theological debates, but
only with the word of God himself. Just as God spoke to
Moses on Sinai, so Jesus speaks now to the disciples. The
Sermon on the Mount is therefore called the "Torah of
the Messiah": the Torah of Moses on Mount Sinai, the
Torah of the Messiah, the Christ, on the Mount of
the Beatitudes. In the Gospel read on Christmas, at the
end of the prologue of John's Gospel, it says: "For the law
was given through Moses; grace and truth came through
Jesus Christ" (Jn 1:17). The connection between the two
mountains has been pointed out often: Mount Sinai, on
which Moses received the word of God, the Torah, and
the Mount of the Beatitudes, where Christ Jesus gave the
Torah of the Messiah. On Sinai God speaks to Moses "face

to face", as it says in the Book of Deuteronomy (Deut 34:10), as he had done with no other human being until then, "as a man speaks to his friend", it says earlier in the Book of Exodus (Ex 33:11).[7] Moses receives instruction, the Torah, directly from God. "This was the only possible source of the Law that was to show Israel its path through history."[8] Moses proclaims the promise at the end of his life: "The LORD your God will raise up for you a prophet like me from among you, from your brethren—him you shall heed" (Deut 18:15).

This promised prophet is Jesus. "It is in Jesus", Pope Benedict says, "that the promise of the new prophet is fulfilled. What was true of Moses only in fragmentary form has now been fully realized in the person of Jesus: He lives before the face of God, not just as a friend, but as a Son; he lives in the most intimate unity with the Father."[9] The teaching of Jesus, the Sermon on the Mount, comes, not from human study, but rather from Jesus' immediate contact with the Father, from the face-to-face dialogue, so to speak, from the vision of him who rests on the Father's bosom (cf. Jn 1:18). The word of Jesus, being the Son's word, is truly God's word. If the words of the Sermon on the Mount were simply a contribution to the ethical debate in Judaism, then or now, then the overriding claim made about them would be utterly exorbitant. No ethicist, no philosopher would dare to appear in public with such a claim: "But I say to you!"

An American rabbi and great Jewish scholar, Jacob Neusner, who has produced the incredible output of several

---

[7] Cf. ibid., 4.
[8] Ibid., 4.
[9] Ibid., 6.

hundred books, wrote the exciting and very interesting book *A Rabbi Talks with Jesus.*[10] He asked Joseph Ratzinger to read the book and to give him a commentary, and he received a reply saying that it is "by far the most important book for the Jewish-Christian dialogue in a long time". Actually, according to the pope, this book prompted him to write his book on Jesus. Rabbi Neusner explains in his book "why, if I had been in the Land of Israel in the first century, I would not have joined the circle of Jesus's disciples." He goes on to write: "I would have dissented, I hope courteously, I am sure with solid reason and argument and fact. If I heard what he said in the Sermon on the Mount, for good and substantive reasons I would not have followed him."[11] He presents the reasons in his book.

Pope Benedict XVI tried to respond to it, likewise with sold reason and argument and fact. This led to a major discussion that goes far beyond the mutual formalities of so many ecumenical dialogues. At issue here is the full seriousness of the question that Neusner poses clearly and decisively: Did the Torah of Moses really need to be reformed? Jesus, Neusner says "claimed to reform and to improve, 'You have heard it said ... but I say ...' *We Jews maintain, and I argue here, that the Torah was and is perfect and beyond improvement, and that Judaism ... was and remains God's will for humanity.* By that criterion I propose to set forth a Jewish dissent to some important teachings of Jesus."[12]

Rabbi Neusner does not merely speak *ex auctoritate*, because the Bible says so, but he also reasons. He also

---

[10] Jacob Neusner, *A Rabbi Talks with Jesus: An Intermillennial, Interfaith Exchange* (New York: Image Books/Doubleday, 1994).

[11] Ibid., xi.

[12] Ibid., xii.

argues that the ways recommended in Jesus' Sermon on the
Mount are problematic in their social and practical consequences. This is precisely the challenge that Pope Benedict
took up: Is it really possible to live out the Sermon on the
Mount? Is it not an unattainable ideal, which on account
of its loftiness discourages rather than encourages? Does it
not promote, precisely because of its loftiness, the hypoc-
risy of which Jesus so often accused the Pharisees and the
scribes and which is certainly flourishing among Christians
also? Rabbi Neusner plainly and honestly decided not to
follow the Rabbi Jesus of Nazareth and not to become
his disciple.

One of the most impressive scenes in the book makes
this clear. Rabbi Neusner mingles among the people who
are listening to Jesus. (From the biblical perspective, we
are, after all, contemporaries and can, so to speak, be
simultaneously present at the events in the Bible.) He sees
the opportunity to speak to Rabbi Jesus himself, to engage
him in conversation, to ask him questions. As he does so,
he also encounters the rich young man, then hears and
experiences Jesus' conversation with him. That evening
he bids Jesus farewell. "We part friends. No ifs, ands, or
buts: just friends."[13] This is the great thing about this book:
he maintains respect and friendship, and yet clearly says
No. Rabbi Neusner then withdraws, I imagine into the
little town of Chorazin, to be alone, to reflect on what
he has heard in prayer and in studying the Torah, so as to
meet the Jewish community and discuss the whole matter
with the local rabbi. In this beautifully imagined scene,
the rabbi asks what he taught, this Rabbi Jesus. Does it

[13] Ibid., 94.

agree with what the rabbis teach? On this subject, Rabbi Neusner says: "I: 'Not exactly, but close.' He: 'What did he leave out?' I: 'Nothing.' He: 'Then what did he add?' I: 'Himself.' "[14] Joseph Ratzinger comments:

> This is the central point where the believing Jew Neusner experiences alarm at Jesus' message, and this is the central reason why he does not wish to follow Jesus, but remains with the "eternal Israel": the centrality of Jesus' "I" in his message, which gives everything a new direction. At this point Neusner cites as evidence of this "addition" Jesus' words to the rich young man: "If you would be perfect, go, sell all you have and come, follow *me*" (cf. Mt 19:21; Neusner, p. 109 [emphasis added]). Perfection, the state of being holy as God is holy (cf. Lev 19:2, 11:44), as demanded by the Torah, now consists in following Jesus.[15]

This is the point where Rabbi Neusner clearly says that, although he will continue to respect him, he will not follow Jesus.

Jesus Himself Is the Torah

Zwi Werblowski, a professor at the Hebrew University in Jerusalem, gave a lecture many years ago at the university in Fribourg and summed up the Jewish-Christian relationship in a brief formula: "What the Torah is for us, Christ is for you!" Yes, for us Christians, Jesus Christ is the embodiment of God's will, the living norm. He is God's Law in

[14] Ibid., 96–97.
[15] Benedict XVI, *Jesus of Nazareth*, 1:105.

person and the Sermon on the Mount in person. He speaks about himself in the Sermon on the Mount and makes it concrete, so to speak, in himself. We can take him as the standard for what is meant in it. But is there not once again a danger of setting a high ideal that cannot be sustained in a daily routine? Or is the Sermon on the Mount situated on another level, as a way of practical everyday living?

The Beatitudes cannot be taken as the constitution for a state. Calling the poor blessed cannot be the basis of social legislation. Just imagine if our finance minister could say: "Blessed are the poor!" "Do not resist the wicked", Jesus says in the Sermon on the Mount. Renouncing resistance against the evil that is done to us cannot be the basis of the penal code. But, on the other hand, we must also say that it would be completely one-sided to maintain that social legislation would be enough to achieve social harmony in our land, in order to practice solidarity with our fellow-man. It would be equally shortsighted to reduce all solutions to interpersonal conflicts to penal law. Something else is needed, too. This requirement that is "more" than commands and prohibitions is precisely the theme of the Sermon on the Mount.

Three select examples should make this clear. I would like first to look at the Beatitudes themselves, then add a word about love of enemy, which is a key to the Sermon on the Mount, and finally to conclude with a reflection about trust in providence: "Do not be anxious."

The chapter on the Beatitudes in the Holy Father's book about Jesus[16] is a masterpiece of scriptural exegesis. The eight Beatitudes in the Sermon on the Mount are

---

[16] Ibid., 64–127.

promises addressed to those in tribulation. The Beatitudes in the Sermon on the Mount consider them, so to speak, not from the perspective of the tribulation, but rather from the perspective of the Father, from God's point of view. All eight formulas are promises expressed in the so-called *passivum divinum*, the divine passive form. Out of reverence for the name of God, the promises are formulated in the passive voice: "Blessed are those who mourn, for they shall be comforted. Blessed are the meek, for they shall inherit the earth", etc. (Mt 5:4–5). This is supposed to express in a discreet, Jewish way: God will comfort them, God will give them the land, God will make them his sons. Pope Benedict comments: "When man begins to see and to live from God's perspective, when he is a companion on Jesus' way, then he lives by new standards, and something of the *éschaton*, of the reality to come, is already present. Jesus brings joy into the midst of affliction."[17] This is the heart of the Beatitudes and Christian experience from the beginning: in the midst of tribulation an indescribable joy (cf. 2 Cor 6:8–10; 4:8–10, 1 Cor 4:9–13), not just in heaven in a perfect way, but even now. Thus Paul, in the midst of his tribulations, can already be a witness to joy. The Beatitudes express what discipleship means. The unmistakable mark of discipleship is joy: "Blessed are the poor in spirit, blessed are the peacemakers, blessed are those who mourn, blessed are those who hunger and thirst for righteousness." This joy is a basic feature of discipleship. Pope Benedict points out that these eight Beatitudes are fulfilled in the person of Jesus himself and are exemplified most clearly in him: they are

[17] Ibid., 72.

a "veiled interior biography of Jesus". Who is the truly
meek man? Who is the truly poor man? He who for our
sake became poor, so as to make us rich with his life. Who
is the man who has a pure heart that sees God?

> Anyone who reads Matthew's text attentively will
> realize that the Beatitudes present a sort of veiled interior
> biography of Jesus, a kind of portrait of his figure. He who
> has no place to lay his head (cf. Mt 8:20) is truly poor; he
> who can say, "Come to me ... for I am meek and lowly
> in heart" (cf. Mt 11:28–29) is truly meek; he is the one
> who is pure of heart and so unceasingly beholds God. He
> is the peacemaker, he is the one who suffers for God's sake.
> The Beatitudes display the mystery of Christ himself, and
> they call us into communion with him. But precisely
> because of their hidden Christological character, the Beat-
> itudes are also a road map for the Church, which recog-
> nizes in them the model of what she herself should be.
> They are directions for discipleship, directions that concern
> every individual, even though—according to the variety
> of callings—they do so differently for each person.[18]

The second example is love of enemy. They say that
this topic is, so to speak, the litmus test of Christian living
and probably the most difficult thing in the Sermon on the
Mount:

> "You have heard that it was said, 'You shall love your
> neighbor and hate your enemy.' But I say to you, Love
> your enemies and pray for those who persecute you, so
> that you may be sons of your Father who is in heaven."
> (Mt 5:43–45)

[18] Ibid., 74.

Love of enemy is no doubt among the most difficult lessons in all of Jesus' preaching. One thing is clear: the commandment to love our enemies cannot replace the penal code. If someone who wrongs his neighbor is then told, "You have earned your victim's love", he certainly gets off too easily. That cannot be a civil law. Is love of enemy a commandment, or it is a counsel? This question has been debated for centuries. Is the Sermon on the Mount made up of commandments or counsels in the first place? Is Jesus recommending to us, or is he commanding us? I find helpful here a traditional distinction that Saint Thomas Aquinas clearly formulated: "Love your enemies" is not only a counsel but a central commandment of Jesus. But Saint Thomas says very plainly: Does love of enemy mean having sympathetic feelings toward one's enemy? That cannot be what is meant. To understand love of enemy in this sense would be perverse and contrary to love, if we had to love our enemies insofar as they are enemies. That cannot be the message. Insofar as they are human beings, however, they must be the object of our love of neighbor. Must we therefore show them signs of affection, also? Often love of neighbor is mistaken for a feeling that I have for the enemy. It does not mean that. It would be unnatural if I had to have feelings of sympathy for my enemy. But I must be willing—and this is a commandment—to respect my enemy as a human being.

The Old Testament Book of Proverbs already says: "If your enemy is hungry, give him bread to eat; and if he is thirsty, give him water to drink" (Prov 25:21).[19] The statement with which Jesus concludes his instruction about

---

[19] Cf. Thomas Aquinas, *Summa Theologiae* II-II, 25, 9 c.

love of enemy goes even farther, of course: "You, therefore, must be perfect, as your heavenly Father is perfect" (Mt 5:48). Therefore, the Sermon on the Mount is about more than what is necessary, about the "something more" that Christ himself accomplished and produced by laying down his life for us "while we were enemies", as the apostle Paul says (Rom 5:10).

A third and final example concerns providence:

> "Therefore I tell you, do not be anxious about your life, what you shall eat or what you shall drink, nor about your body, what you shall put on.... Look at the birds of the air.... Your heavenly Father feeds them.... Therefore do not be anxious about tomorrow, for tomorrow will be anxious for itself." (Mt 6:25–26, 34)

This is not a platform for social legislation. Nor will we say to those in need, as James writes (describing an example not to be followed), "Go in peace, be warmed and filled", without helping them (Jas 2:16). This is not a guide for preparing a budget at the governmental or the personal level. It is not a license for inaction and negligence; rather, it is the experience of the school of discipleship on the way with Jesus. It is about developing a relationship of trust with the Father: "Your heavenly Father knows that you need [all these things]." The Sermon on the Mount is Jesus' school of life, in which he himself is the model and teacher. He lived constantly in this trust.

Will I manage to do that? Is this whole thing not an excessive demand? Will I ever succeed in living according to the Sermon on the Mount? Is Jesus an unattainable example? If we read the Sermon on the Mount simply as a stricter law, then we are discouraged from the start. We shall not achieve it by our own willpower. But the Sermon on the Mount is not an especially rigorous moral code; rather, it is—as Saint Thomas says so beautifully— "the new law of the Gospel", the *lex nova evangelii.*

Every person already carries the Ten Commandments in his heart, i n his conscience. They are written not so much on stone tablets as on our heart, on our conscience (cf. *CCC* 580). The Sermon on the Mount, Saint Thomas says, is written on our heart by the Holy Spirit. It becomes an interior law of living, a law that moves us from within. Jesus himself places it into our heart, and the more we walk along the way with him, the more he will conform us to his own life by his Holy Spirit and become himself the law of the new life within us. Only in this manner does Christian living acquire the power to convince others. Jesus not only taught the Sermon on the Mount but also lived it, and by his Spirit he has inscribed it on the hearts of his disciples.

V

"I Came to Call Sinners"

Is Jesus' School of Life Only for the Righteous?

When Jesus called the tax collector Matthew, also known as Levi, to follow him and attended a banquet with his friends and colleagues, there were vehement protests from the Pharisees: "Why does your teacher eat with tax collectors and sinners?" they asked the disciples of Jesus.

> But when he heard it, he said, "Those who are well have no need of a physician, but those who are sick. Go and learn what this means, 'I desire mercy, and not sacrifice.' For I came not to call the righteous, but sinners." (Mt 9:9–13).

Does this mean that only sinners are qualified to follow Jesus? Are the only ones eligible for his school of life those who are sinners or who recognize and acknowledge that they are sinners? Do the righteous have no place at all among Jesus' followers? Jesus called people to *conversion*. Sinners have gone astray and taken the wrong paths. They must turn back, because they are headed for destruction. That is clear. Jesus' call to conversion is urgent. "Turn around, when possible", the GPS says, when we are driving in the wrong direction. Tirelessly Jesus points out the necessity of conversion; there is still time for it. It will not be long now; soon you will stand before your judge. Be reconciled quickly with your opponent while you are on the way (cf. Mt 5:25–26; Lk 12:58–59). "At any moment the cry may ring out: the bridegroom is coming; then the wedding procession will go with torches into the banqueting hall and the doors will be shut, irrevocably. Take care that you have oil for your torch (Matt. 25.1–12). In a word, repent, while there is still time."[1]

Who has to convert? When Jesus speaks about those "who have no need of conversion", does he mean it ironically? In the parable of the lost sheep he says: "Just so, I tell you, there will be more joy in heaven over one sinner who repents than over ninety-nine righteous persons who need no repentance" (Lk 15:7). Does Jesus mean here those who imagine that they are righteous? Or does he mean it without irony?

I find different interpretations by two exegetes whom I greatly admire. Joachim Jeremias (d. 1979), a Protestant exegete and an outstanding expert on the Jewish world in which Jesus lived, writes:

> Repentance is necessary not only for so-called sinners but also, indeed even more, for those who in the world's view "need no repentance" (Lk 15.7), for the upright and the pious, who have committed no great sin. Repentance is most urgent for them.[2]

[1] Joachim Jeremias, *New Testament Theology*, vol. 1 (New York: Scribner, 1971), 152.

[2] Ibid.

Adolf Schlatter, on the other hand, is convinced that Jesus is not speaking ironically about the righteous when he mentions them in contrast with sinners:

> We do not arrive at an understanding of what Jesus was doing if we empty the term "righteous" of its meaning, so that it no longer seriously denotes moral approval. If it is used ironically, then the condemnation of the sinners whom Jesus contrasts to the righteous also loses its seriousness. The sick whom he spoke about were in his opinion genuinely sick; the healthy were just as certainly healthy. Jesus acknowledged that the righteous really obeyed God and did what he commanded.... Anyone who attenuates this judgment ends up idealizing the sin in the other part of the contrast, which falsifies Jesus' intention.[3]

Jesus rejoiced over genuinely righteous persons, whether Nathanael, whom Jesus called "a man without guile" (cf. Jn 1:48), or the pagan Roman centurion about whom Jesus said, "Not even in Israel have I found such faith" (Mt 8:10). Jesus not only called sins by their name but even wept over them (cf. Lk 19:41). Precisely because sin is man's deepest misery, Jesus wanted to lead sinners to repentance and to convert them to true righteousness: "Unless your righteousness exceeds that of the scribes and Pharisees, you will never enter the kingdom of heaven" (Mt 5:20).

Sinners are supposed to convert to this far greater righteousness. And only in this way can we be disciples of Jesus. The sinner's conversion is Jesus' great desire. In repentance it becomes evident where Jesus wants to lead us: "You ... must be perfect, as your heavenly Father is perfect" (Mt 5:48). The major motive for conversion

---

[3] Adolf Schlatter, *Die Geschichte des Christus* (Stuttgart, 1921), 190; cited in *THWNT* I:333.

is God's joy over every child of Eve who turns back from sin and from wandering in the shadow of death (cf. Lk 1:79) and finds his way home to the Father.

> Repentance is joy that God is so gracious. Even more, repentance is *God's* joy (Luke 15.7, 10). God rejoices like the shepherd who rediscovers a stray animal, or the woman who rediscovers her lost coin, or the father who rediscovers his lost son ..., like "the bridegroom [who rejoices] over the bride" (Isa. 62.5).... Because repentance means being able to live from forgiveness, being able to be a child again, repentance is joy.[4]

God's joy over our homecoming is the motive for Jesus' call to conversion. God's sorrow and wrath, if we may use these biblical images, are expressions of the tragedy of sin. Because not one soul is supposed to be lost, God goes after the sinner who is on the path to destruction. Because God wants his children to live, he did his utmost: he gave his Son over to death in order to "deliver us from the dominion of darkness" (cf. Col 1:13). This makes clear, however, "what a great burden sin is".[5] What does this mean for discipleship, for Jesus' school of life?

"He Will Save His People from Their Sins"

Even the name "Jesus" has to do with sin. As the angel announced to Joseph: "You shall call his name Jesus, for

---

[4] Jeremias, *New Testament Theology*, 1:158.

[5] See Anselm of Canterbury, *Cur Deus homo* I, 21, cited in English from: *Why God Became Man*, trans. Joseph M. Colleran (Albany, N.Y.: Magi Books, 1969), 108ff.; cf. Christoph Cardinal Schönborn, *Jesus nachfolgen im Alltag: Impulse zur Vertiefung des Glaubens* (Freiburg im Breisgau, 2004), 117–18.

he will save his people from their sins" (Mt 1:21). Zechariah, filled with the Spirit, says about his son John, the future Baptist: "[You will] give knowledge of salvation to his people in the forgiveness of their sins" (Lk 1:77).

Following Christ, Jesus' school of life, is not only about imitating Christ (*imitatio Christi*) as the great example. First, it is about the experience of redemption, about becoming whole. It is about liberation from sin, redemption, release from the fetters of sin, ransom (so to speak) from captivity to the Evil One.

Nothing about Jesus' ministry and teaching was more convincing than the real, visible, tangible change for the better that could be observed in the people who had met Jesus. So it is to this day. Words rarely make people curious about Jesus, even though they—being the word of God that is proclaimed—are not without their effect. What convinces most is a way of life. When it becomes evident that Jesus really changes lives, makes people alive and radiant, this speaks for itself. Then Jesus' school of life becomes "the experience of salvation".

The Forgiveness of Sins: The Heart of Jesus' Mission

When John the Baptist saw Jesus walk by, he said to his disciples: "Behold, the Lamb of God, who takes away the sin of the world" (Jn 1:29). What does "sin of the world" mean in the singular, in this comprehensive dimension: the sin *of the world*? What does *sin* mean in the first place? Of what does it consist? How is it manifested? How is it perceived, exposed? And then: How is it *taken away*? What does this taking away accomplish? "He will save his people from their sins": How is this manifested, what consequences does this have for the individual and for his people?

In the first days of his public ministry in Capernaum and the vicinity, Jesus drove out many demons and worked many cures. The disciples especially remembered one healing, probably because it was particularly spectacular (cf. Mk 2:1–12): Four men were carrying a paralyzed man. They could not get to Jesus; a dense crowd was standing in the way. So without hesitation they climbed onto the flat roof of the house, removed some of the tiles, made a hole in the ceiling, and lowered the pallet—probably on ropes—right in front of Jesus. "And when Jesus saw their faith, he said to the paralytic, 'Child, your sins are forgiven'" (Mk 2:5). Jesus knew the thoughts of some of those present, who were saying to themselves: This is unheard of! What is this Jesus saying? God alone can forgive sins! Jesus certainly knew that, and for us this is an important point in understanding what sin means. Jesus did not dispute the fact that God alone can forgive sins. But he claimed to have this authority: he, the "Son of man", as he called himself. And to confirm this, he healed the paralytic by his word alone.

Here we are confronted with Jesus' claim to be able to forgive sins. That is why he came. That is the mission already contained in his name. The healing of the paralytic, though, says something not only about Jesus' divine authority, but also about human misery. The first thing that Jesus grants the paralyzed man is the forgiveness of his sins. Jesus does not say that he was paralyzed on account of his sins. Paralysis is not a punishment from God. Rather, Jesus shows the correct sequence: the first thing of which we must be healed, which is more important than all bodily healing, is the wound of sin. A man can be physically fit as a fiddle yet "suffer the loss of his own soul" (Mt 16:26, Douay-Rheims) because of his sins.

The encounter with Jesus, with "the Holy One of God" (as the terrified demons call him in Mark 1:24), becomes the moving experience of one's own sinfulness. So it was for the first apostles, when they encountered Jesus' holiness firsthand. After an unsuccessful night of fishing, at Jesus' command they cast their nets once again and caught so many fish that the boats were about to sink. "When Simon Peter saw it, he fell down at Jesus' knees, saying, 'Depart from me, for I am a sinful man'" (Lk 5:8). Holy fear seized him and his companions when they were face to face with Jesus.

When we encounter holiness, the consequence is a deep, interior fear. So it was for me when I met Padre Pio in 1961. This was my experience when I was close to people who were imbued with the holiness of God. Isaiah had the same experience in the Temple when he had a vision of God's glory: "Woe is me! For I am lost; for I am a man of unclean lips,... for my eyes have seen the King, the LORD of hosts!" (Is 6:5).

The experience of one's own sinfulness in the presence of holiness is difficult to describe, but it is an unforgettable gift. It is not so much a feeling of fear of being condemned, nor is it shame over one's own inadequacy. It is something frightening and gladdening at the same time: fear of the greatness and gladness about the incomparable closeness of God. At the same time, it is a sense of being incomprehensibly accepted and the disturbing perception of one's own—and this is the only word that fits—one's *own* sins.

Again Luke, the especially sensitive evangelist, is the one who records this moment in which Peter encounters the holiness of his Master. At Peter's third betrayal we read:

And immediately, while he was still speaking, the cock crowed. And the Lord turned and looked at Peter. And Peter remembered the word of the Lord, how he had said to him, "Before the cock crows today, you will deny me three times." And he went out and wept bitterly. (Lk 22:60–62)

What sin really means can probably be measured only by such experiences. In the hymn by Saint Ambrose, which is sung in some editions of the Church's Liturgy of the Hours on Sunday, it says:

> *Jesu, labantes respice*
> *Et nos videndo corrige;*
> *Si respicis, labes cadunt*
> *Fletuque culpa solvitur.*

> Jesu! look on us when we fall;
> One momentary glance of thine
> Can from her guilt the soul recall
> To tears of penitence divine.

From the naming of Jesus after his birth ("... for he will save his people from their sins") until the anticipation of his death on the Cross even before his Passion, his whole life stands under the banner of the forgiveness of sins:

And he took a chalice, and when he had given thanks he gave it to them, saying, "Drink of it, all of you; for this is my blood of the covenant, which is poured out for many for the forgiveness of sins." (Mt 26:27–28)

What Is Sin?

When we ask about sin, let us draw on the storehouse of the Church's experience: it includes theological reflection and attempts in catechesis and in theology to comprehend the phenomenon "sin" more precisely and to find adequate concepts for it. What does the *Catechism of the Catholic Church* say about the subject? It is "a valid and legitimate instrument for ecclesial communion and a sure norm for teaching the faith" (Pope John Paul II).[6] One definition by Saint Augustine says: Sin is "an utterance, a deed, or a desire contrary to the eternal law".[7] The *Catechism* explains this definition:

> Sin is an offense against reason, truth, and right conscience; it is a failure in genuine love for God and neighbor caused by a perverse attachment to certain goods. It wounds the nature of man and injures human solidarity.[8]

It is surprising that the *Catechism* describes sin first as *an offense against reason*. In saying this, it echoes a view familiar to extra-biblical, non-Christian thought: "Whoever says moral failure [sin] is a kind of disorder—and one that brings further disorder in its wake—is no doubt saying something important [about the human condition]" (Josef Pieper).[9]

Sin, in Greek *hamartia*, in Latin *peccatum*, means first of all a mistake. Something has missed the mark. "Any act

---

[6] John Paul II, Apostolic Constitution *Fidei depositum* (October 11, 1992), 3.

[7] Augustine, *Contra Faustum* 22:PL42:418; cited in *CCC* 1849; cf. Thomas Aquinas, *Summa theologiae* I-II, q. 71, a. 6.

[8] *CCC* 1849.

[9] Josef Pieper, *Concept of Sin*, trans. Edward T. Oakes (South Bend, Ind.: St. Augustine's Press, 2001), 48.

that lacks order ... may be called an error [*peccatum*]", says Thomas Aquinas.[10] We speak, for instance, about traffic offenses or environmental sins. Artistic mistakes and mistakes of every sort are called *peccatum* in Latin. It is unreasonable not to follow the instructions for using a product. Even before the moral question is posed, whether or not someone made a mistake deliberately, it is fundamentally true that mistakes are unreasonable, because they miss a target. The financial crisis clearly shows this. Here things became ends in themselves—in a way that is clearly recognizable in retrospect—and this mistake developed to the point of absurdity. The financial market distanced itself more and more from the real economy and became increasingly virtual, until the bubble burst. One municipal authority in Austria, for example, at the advice of the local bank director, sold the debts of the municipality to Canada in order to make a profit on them. After 2008, the municipality had nothing left but its own debts and the considerable losses in Canada. That is not a unique case; that was (and to some extent still is) the system: *peccatum*—missing the mark, sheer unreason. But is what the mayor and the bank director did a sin? Did they know what they were doing? Is something a sin even if I do not recognize it at all as such? Knowing about the sinfulness of a mistake is part of sin, is it not?

That is why the *Catechism* goes on to say that sin is an *offense against truth*. Much of what is "not in order" has to do with the fact that we do not realize what the order is. We are mistaken, deceive ourselves, are deceived, let ourselves be deceived, suppress the truth, refuse to acknowledge it.

[10] Thomas Aquinas, *De malo* 2, 2.

They can print on the cigarette package as big and bold as they want: "Smoking is dangerous to your health", and people will still smoke heavily. We all know that twisting and distorting the truth causes great harm, is detrimental to the lives of other people, indeed, and can even cause permanent injury. Yet not a day goes by without our twisting things or not keeping strictly to the truth, even if only in little things. Sin has a lot to do with untruth; it is always a lie, also. Reason and truth are injured, denied; that is why so much is not "in order".

Sin, the *Catechism* says, is also an *offense against right conscience*. Josef Pieper writes that sin is an erroneous action "contrary to better knowledge and thus against one's con-*science*".[11] An unintentional mistake that has serious consequences can torture us for a long time. We reproach ourselves and wish too late that we had been more careful. But only when there is a moral failing does another dimension come into play: the judgment of our conscience. In his commentary on the story of Joseph in the Book of Genesis, Saint John Chrysostom speaks about this with regard to the brothers who sold him into slavery in Egypt and who now stand before him, asking for help, without recognizing him. Now, in their own fear and distress, they remember what they had done to their brother then:

> Now, notice at this point, I ask you, how conscience, that incorruptible judge, rises up against them, without anyone accusing them or bringing them to book, and how they turn their own accusers.... This, you see, is what sin is like: when it is done and takes effect, then it shows the excess of its own impropriety.... When it is committed, it

---

[11] Pieper, *Concept of Sin*, 48.

clouds the mind, and like a dense fog it blinds the intellect, but later conscience is stirred and flays the mind unmercifully with every kind of accusation, highlighting the impropriety of what was done.[12]

Sin is an offense against reason, truth, and conscience. Augustine said that it is a deed "contrary to the eternal law", in other words, to the order that the Creator inscribed in his creation, which we recognize by the light of reason and are able to do with our free will.

But is that really all? Does that describe the tragedy of sin sufficiently? The *Catechism* goes a step farther: "Sin is an offense against God" (*CCC* 1850). Sin is also an offense against human morality, but first it is *aversio a Deo*, turning away from God. Here lies the core of what sin is and means: "Against you, you only, have I sinned, and done that which is evil in your sight" (Ps 51:4). Sin is first and most intrinsically turning away from God. This constitutes its importance and its gravity. This makes the price of liberation from sin so high: "Sin sets itself against God's love for us and turns our hearts away from it" (*CCC* 1850).

Do I really rebel against God when I sin? Do I deliberately will this, with a full understanding of what I am doing? Is our sinning not often a kind of ignorance, a sort of blindness? We are not at all aware of the depth of our failings. After all, Jesus prayed for his judges and their henchmen: "Father, forgive them; for they know not what they do" (Lk 23:34). Do we know what we are doing when we sin? Do we really want to "grieve God"

---

[12] John Chrysostom, *Homilies on Genesis*, 74, 2–3, trans. Robert C. Hill, Fathers of the Church 87 (Washington, D.C.: CUA Press, 1986–1992), 228–29.

or "offend" him? Can a man grieve God in the first place?
Can he offend him?

Here Saint Augustine, probably based on his own dra-
matic life experience and on his great familiarity with
Sacred Scripture, tried to elaborate the innermost core
of what constitutes sin. In his work *The City of God*, he
sees two kinds of life in conflict with each other: self-love
and the love of God; self-love, which "dared to despise
even God", and love of God, which "is ready to tram-
ple on self".[13] Josef Pieper formulates it as an alternative
facing man: "He can either choose himself or God." And
he explains: "The true alternative ... looks like this: *either
self-realization as surrender to God by recognizing one's
own creatureliness; or* 'absolute' self-love by trying to realize oneself by denying or ignoring one's creatureliness."[14]
The innermost nature of sin is "me, me, me!"—absolute
self-love, trying to be "like God" (Gen 3:5). It is *superbia*,
pride, according to tradition.

Here the objection arises again: Does this radical sin exist
at all "in its pure form"? Does our human sin not always
consist of an inextricable tangle of weaknesses, ignorance,
heedlessness, neglect, and forgetfulness? That is what the
thicket of sin is made of. When are we ever so radically
wicked that we would totally refuse to obey God in an act
that involves us completely?

This leads to the question: Is there such a thing as a
"deadly sin" (for that is how we should translate the classi-
cal concept of *peccatum mortale* literally)? For many people,

[13] Augustine, *De civitate Dei*, 14, 28, cited from *The City of God: An Abridged
Version* (New York: Image Books, 1958), 321; cf. *CCC* 1850, which translates
more literally: "love of oneself even to contempt of God".

[14] Pieper, *Concept of Sin*, 64.

the seriousness of deadly sin has probably been lost because so many things were hastily identified as mortal sins.

We recognize what tradition, with all its experience, means by "deadly sin" by looking at the other part of the distinction, so-called "venial sin".

> One commits *venial sin* when, in a less serious matter, he does not observe the standard prescribed by the moral law, or when he disobeys the moral law in a grave matter, but without full knowledge or without complete consent.[15]

No doubt this description applies to most of our sins. They are weaknesses rather than truly wicked deeds deliberately done. But in this the tragedy of sin is once again evident. Let us cite Augustine again:

> So long as a person bears flesh, he cannot but have some at least slight sins. But don't belittle what we are referring to as these slight sins. If you belittle them when you weigh them, shudder when you count them out. For many slight ones make a great one: many drops fill a river; many grains make a mass. And what hope is there? Confession above all.[16]

What distresses me about the phenomenon of so-called "venial sin" was described as follows by the visionary on Patmos in his letter to the Christian community in Ephesus: "But I have this against you, that you have abandoned the love you had at first" (Rev 2:4). And shortly before

---

[15] *CCC* 1862; cf. *CCC* 1863.

[16] Augustine, *Homilies on the First Epistle of John*, introduction, translation, and notes by Boniface Ramsey, in *The Works of Saint Augustine: A Translation for the 21st Century*, pt. 3, vol. 14 (Brooklyn, N.Y.: New City Press, 2008), 26–27.

his Passion, our Lord said: "And because wickedness is multiplied, most men's love will grow cold. But he who endures to the end will be saved" (Mt 24:12–13).

This "cooling of love" is the real tragedy of sin, the hardening of hearts. It is already the death of the soul. It is most dangerous when it causes love to die in the innermost recesses of the heart. This hardening can occur through several small stages: inattentive, unloving, and on and on and on. Then the heart becomes hardened. That is the tragedy of "deadly sin".

What can guard us against it? It requires the one who "takes away the sin of the world" (Jn 1:29), and it requires his Spirit, who "will convince the world of sin" (Jn 16:8). In his profound meditation on this saying of Jesus, Pope John Paul II shows that the Holy Spirit will convict the world of sin, that the Spirit can show us the truth of our sin, not in order to accuse us, but to save us; not to expose the sins, but to heal the sinner.[17] The Holy Spirit reveals to us our sins and at the same time the forgiveness of them. For we first learn what sin really is in the presence of the love of Christ. Maybe that is the reason why the saints had the most profound awareness of being sinners. Only in Jesus' school of life does sin become comprehensible in its full dimensions. Only in the grace of forgiveness is it possible to sense how abysmal it would be to be separated from God as a result of sin. So we can only ask Jesus, in his mercy, for the grace that the priest prays for silently before Communion: "Never let me be parted from you."

---

[17] Cf. John Paul II, Encyclical *Dominum et vivificantem*, 27.

VI

"He Who Does Not Take His Cross ..."

The Cross: The Key to Jesus' School of Life

"If any man would come after me, let him deny himself and take up his cross and follow me" (Mt 16:24). Discipleship means following the way of the Cross. Jesus leaves no doubt about that, but the question arises: Is that also the reason why so few people follow him? If discipleship means following the way of the Cross, one is tempted to say: Lord, do not be surprised that so few follow you! At least that is how Thomas à Kempis saw it in his *Imitatio Christi*, the "Imitation of Christ". He writes:

> Jesus today has many who love his heavenly kingdom, but few who carry his cross; many who yearn for comfort, few who long for distress. Plenty of people he finds to share his banquet, few to share his fast. Every one desires to take part in his rejoicing, but few are willing to suffer anything for his sake. There are ... many that revere his miracles, few that follow him in the indignity of his cross; many that love Jesus as long as nothing runs counter to them; many that praise and bless him, as long as they receive some comfort from him; but should Jesus hide from them and

leave them for a while, they fall to complaining or become deeply depressed.[1]

These are sober, skeptical words. Yes, the saying about the Cross is frightening. But we console ourselves by saying that it was for the apostles, too. Jesus' prophecies of his Passion met with incomprehension and fear. Obviously Jesus confronted his Passion and Cross decisively. Luke says at one point that Jesus (literally) "set his face to go to Jerusalem" (Lk 9:51). He walked resolutely toward his Passion. Mark reminds us that those who were following him, his disciples, were afraid (Mk 9:32). So it is with many of us; the cross frightens us. Following Christ can be sinister. Jesus left no doubt about that. He is not talking about a pleasant stroll when he says to his disciples: "Behold, I send you out as sheep in the midst of wolves" (Mt 10:16; Lk 10:3). At the Last Supper, in the solemnity and holiness of that hour, he says:

> "Remember the word that I said to you, 'A servant is not greater than his master.' If they persecuted me, they will persecute you; if they kept my word, they will keep yours also." (Jn 15:20)

Love the Cross

Being a disciple of Jesus means having a share in his destiny: in the Cross but also in the Resurrection. Moreover, the Cross holds a central place. But is the Cross really the

[1] Thomas à Kempis, *The Imitation of Christ*, trans. Ronald Knox and Michael Oakley, II, 11, 1 (New York: Sheed & Ward, 1959), 88.

centerpiece of our faith? The Cross is and remains a horror. The people of Jesus' time knew that; they spoke about the *mors turpissima crucis*, the "most shameful death on the cross" (Tacitus),[2] or they called this death penalty, a practice that dated back to pre-Roman times, *crudelissimum terrimumque supplicium*, the "most cruel and terrible execution" (Cicero).[3] Jesus died this death. He was one of the countless men who were tortured to death in this cruel, inhumane *supplicium*, this execution. And we are supposed to love it? Love the Cross? Embrace the Cross? Very early on there was mockery of the Cross. Again and again German intellectuals like to cite mocking verses by Goethe:

> I can tolerate much. Most troublesome things I bear
> With a calm demeanor, just as God commands me.
> A few things, though, repel me like poison or a snake,
> Four: tobacco smoke, bugs, garlic and +.[4]

It is as odious as garlic and tobacco. Again and again the Cross is mocked in caricatures, but that is nothing new. A mocking graffito in Rome from early Christian times depicts a crucified man with a donkey's head, and scratched underneath are the words: "So-and-so worships his god." Paul knew that the Cross was a scandal: "For Jews demand signs and Greeks seek wisdom, but we preach Christ crucified, a stumbling block to Jews and folly to Gentiles" (1 Cor 1:22–23).

"If any man would come after me, let him deny himself and take up his cross and follow me" (Mt 16:24). Do we

---

[2] Tacitus, *Historiae* IV, 3, 11.
[3] Cicero, *Orationes in Verrem* V, 65, 165.
[4] Goethe, *Venezianische Epigramme*, no. 66 (1790 version).

want to do that? Can I want to take up my cross? Is that not sick, morbid, unnatural? Saint John Chrysostom interpreted this saying of Jesus in his Commentary on Matthew:

> "If any man will come after me." "I force not, I compel not, but each one I make lord of his own choice; wherefore also I say, 'If any man will.' For to good things do I call you, not to things evil, or burdensome; not to punishment and vengeance, that I should have to compel. Nay, the nature of the thing is alone sufficient to attract you."
>
> Now, thus saying, He [Jesus] drew them unto Him the more. For he indeed that uses compulsion often turns men away.... For soothing is a mightier thing than force. Wherefore even He Himself said, "If any man will." "For great," saith He, "are the good things which I give you, and such as for men even to run to them of their own accord...." Wherefore Christ compels [us] not.[5]

Therefore this is about good things. To desire the Cross? To regard the Cross as something good? No one is compelled to follow Jesus, and therefore no one has to take up his Cross either. But what motivates me? "What is in it for me?" This question is often asked, especially by young people. What do I get out of it? Why should I make the effort to follow the way of the Cross? During the City Mission in 2003, I asked Sister Elvira a question. This magnificent Italian nun founded the community *Cenacolo*,[6] which by now has foundations throughout the world to take in drug-addicted boys and girls and to enable them to make a fresh start. Many, many profound healings have been made possible in this community through God's help. Full of Joy, Sister Elvira gave a thrilling talk about Christ and about the healing that he grants. I asked her: How can I love the cross? And she answered immediately and clearly: "Not the cross, but the Crucified!"

It is not about loving the cross but, rather, loving the Crucified. He is the one we are supposed to follow. We are to be united with the Crucified and Risen One, with his suffering and with his love. Because he took up his Cross, I want to be with him and take up my cross. This little saying was the key: He loved me to the extreme! That is why the cross acquires an entirely new, powerful meaning. He, the Crucified, gives the cross a new meaning. If the cross that I have to carry gets its meaning from him, then I can say, like Saint John Chrysostom, that the cross becomes something good, a gain, because it unites me with him. But "the natural man"—Paul would say "the carnal man"—does not see that. For him, the cross is simply absurdity, sorrow, destruction, something worthless. But there is the experience of looking at it in a different way, so that the Cross of Christ and our cross appear in a different light with him. In the abstract, that is quite incomprehensible. You have to experience the fact that the cross can be something good, a grace.

An example from the life of Saint Teresa Benedicta of the Cross, O.C.D., Saint Edith Stein (d. 1942), should illustrate this. She was from an orthodox Jewish family from Breslau, but as a girl she decided to become an agnostic and stopped praying. She says: "I very deliberately and freely decided to give up praying." After passing her final school examinations brilliantly, she began to study philosophy with Edmund Husserl, the great German-Jewish philosopher. One of her fellow students, Adolf Reinach, who was very happily married at a young age, fell in 1917 in the First World War. Professor Husserl sent Edith Stein to visit Reinach's widow with instructions to look through his philosophical papers with her and to help her. Edith was very frightened by this commission. She set out on this journey with great worry and anxiety. Reinach had meant a lot to her, personally as a colleague, but also as a man, with his kindness and integrity. She herself had been painfully affected by her colleague's death and imagined how she might bring some consolation to the mourning widow. But the situation turned out to be completely different. Instead of encountering a broken, disconsolate woman, as she had expected, she met a woman who was a consolation to her friends more than she herself expected consolation.

Looking back on this surprising meeting, Edith Stein writes:

> It was my first encounter with the cross and with the divine power that it imparts to those who carry it. I saw for the first time the Church, born from Christ's redemptive suffering, in her victory over the sting of death palpably in front of me. It was the moment when my disbelief broke down, Judaism paled, and Christ shone forth: Christ in the mystery of the Cross.[7]

Christ in the mystery of the Cross became for Edith Stein the center of her life and of her death. She saw firsthand in the widow of her colleague and friend Adolf Reinach "that the most basic experience of her faith is founded

[7] Cited in: Elisabeth Otto, *Welt—Person—Gott: Eine Untersuchung zur theologischen Grundlage der Mystik bei Edith Stein* (Vallendar-Schönstatt, 1990), 107.

on the death and Resurrection of Jesus. Edith Stein can observe in her that the human being who believes in Jesus Christ understands history in terms of him, that he interprets it in terms of the mystery of the Cross, which is to say: in terms of the mystery of God's love."[8] Father Hirschmann, S.J., recalls after the war the last conversation that he had with Edith Stein, Sister Teresa Benedicta of the Cross, in the Carmel in Echt, Holland, shortly before her deportation to Auschwitz. He writes:

> The decisive reason for her conversion to Christianity was, as she related to me, the manner in which her friend Frau Reinach offered, by the power of the mystery of the Cross, the sacrifice that had been imposed on her by her husband's death at the front during the First World War. In this sacrifice she experienced a proof of the truth of the Christian religion and was made amenable to it. (Letter dated May 13, 1950)[9]

The final step leading to the conversion of Edith Stein and thus to her baptism was her reading of the autobiography of Saint Teresa of Avila. "Teresa showed Edith Stein the cross as the source of life. This source becomes fruitful for her in her love for the Crucified One and in following him."[10]

Love for the Crucified One

Following Christ, discipleship, and Jesus' school of life can mean only one thing: love for the Crucified One.

[8] Ibid.
[9] Ibid.
[10] Ibid., 110.

For on the Cross Jesus proved the fullness of his love. "Greater love has no man than this, that a man lay down his life for his friends", Jesus says after the Last Supper (Jn 15:13). Edith Stein once wrote to her fellow student and close friend Roman Ingarden: "Where experience of one's own is lacking, one must be guided by testimonies of *homines religiosi* [believers]. Indeed, there is no lack of them" (Letter dated November 20, 1927).[11] If you have not had this experience yourself, you should look at and listen to those who have had it. One of the very important tasks facing the Church today is to learn how to tell about these experiences. The Church is a storytelling community. We should tell stories like the one about Edith Stein, but also stories from our own life. That is the most decisive thing about mission. This means, not collaring someone and boring him, but, rather, telling him what we have experienced or letting those who have experienced it tell about it.

The *Science of the Cross* (the title of Edith Stein's last work, which was completed shortly before her arrest on August 2, 1942) is focused entirely on following the way of the cross, as Edith Stein saw it exemplified in the life of Saint John of the Cross (d. 1591). She finds in John of the Cross a very specially privileged witness to the learning experience in Jesus' school of life, the experience of "the science of the cross". He is for her a teacher who had only one goal: "'conformity with the beloved' in all his phases: life, Passion, agony, death, and Resurrection".[12]

---

[11] Edith Stein, *Gesamtausgabe* (Freiburg im Breisgau: Herder, 2000–), vol. 4, letter 117.

[12] Introduction by Fr. Ulrich Dobhan, O.C.D., to Edith Stein, *Kreuzeswissenschaft*, in *Gesamtausgabe*, vol. 18, xxif.

This "conformity with the beloved" is the fundamental experience of a saint like John of the Cross and, likewise, of Saint Paul, a Jew like Edith Stein, but a believing Jew, not one who was religiously aloof as she was. He describes himself as a law-abiding Jew (Gal 1:14) and says that he has "seen Jesus our Lord" (1 Cor 9:1), that God "was pleased to reveal his Son" to him (Gal 1:16). This Paul, who met Jesus on the road to Damascus, is completely and utterly focused on his love for the Crucified. All he wants now is to know Christ and to proclaim "Christ crucified" (1 Cor 1:23). One senses in his letters his passionate dedication to Christ and his Cross. For him "to live is Christ, and to die is gain" (Phil 1:21). This is expressed above all in the Letter to the Galatians, which is a sort of little "autobiography" of the apostle:

> I have been crucified with Christ; it is no longer I who live, but Christ who lives in me; and the life I now live in the flesh I live by faith in the Son of God, who loved me and gave himself for me. (Gal 2:20)

Paul, who did not know Jesus personally, can say: "He loved me and gave himself for me." He, who did not know Jesus, recognizes that Jesus knew him, even before he encountered him. "Saul, Saul, why do you persecute me?" So he addresses him; he knows him (Acts 9:4). Paul's major concern is that the disciples of Jesus might evade the cross, and try to remove the "stumbling block of the cross" (Gal 5:11) and to avoid persecution "for the cross of Christ" (Gal 6:12). The reader senses here the apostle's deep sorrow that Christians turn aside from the cross: "Many, of whom I have often told you and now tell you

even with tears, walk as enemies of the cross of Christ.
Their end is destruction, their god is the belly, and they
glory in their shame, with minds set on earthly things"
(Phil 3:18–19). Paul is not saying that about the pagans; he
is saying that about his brothers and sisters.

"To walk as enemies of the cross of Christ" is the worst
thing that can happen to a disciple of Christ. For then he
betrays Jesus, just as Peter betrayed his Master in the court-
yard of the high priest (cf. Lk 22:61–62). But how are we to
become friends of Christ's Cross? Like Edith Stein on her
journey to conversion, we too should look at those who
walk as friends of Christ's Cross. Paul says this simply but
valiantly: "Brethren, join in imitating me, and mark those
who so walk as you have an example in us" (Phil 3:17).

When this verse is translated precisely, it is even more
beautiful: "Become my fellow imitators." Just as I imitate
Christ, so become with me, following my example, imitators of Christ. To become friends of Christ's Cross means
to become imitators of Christ: "Have this mind among
yourselves, which was in Christ Jesus", Paul says in the
Letter to the Philippians (Phil 2:5). Love for the Crucified
is love for him whom we have the privilege of imitating,
who by his life showed us what it means to be a friend
of the Cross. What this way of thinking looks like was
summed up very early on by the communities of the primitive Church in a hymn. It is one of the best-known early
Christian hymns, and we sing it today in the Church's
Liturgy of the Hours every Saturday at Evening Prayer:

> Though he was in the form of God,
> [Christ] did not count equality with God a thing
>   to be grasped,

but emptied himself,
taking the form of a servant, being born in the
　　likeness of men.
And being found in human form
he humbled himself and became obedient
unto death, even death on a cross.
Therefore God has highly exalted him
and bestowed on him the name
which is above every name,
that at the name of Jesus every knee should bow,
in heaven and on earth and under the earth,
and every tongue confess
that Jesus Christ is Lord,
to the glory of God the Father. (Phil 2:6–11)

The Cross and Self-Denial

The first condition for being a "friend of Christ's Cross" is obedience. This means "dying" to one's own will, as Christ did in the Garden of Olives when he insistently asked his Father: "Let this chalice pass from me; nevertheless, not as I will, but as you will" (Mt 26:39). How far the disciples still were from this obedience is plain from the fact that they were sleeping in the Garden of Gethsemane, while Jesus prayed in agony (cf. Mt 26:36–46).

"If any man would come after me, let him deny himself and take up his cross and follow me." Someone who does not deny himself cannot be a friend of Christ's Cross. But what does self-denial mean? On this subject there is a lot of spiritual literature, the experience down through the centuries, from the writings of the monastic fathers down through the great Carmelite masters to the present day. I came upon a sermon on self-denial by the young Blessed John Henry Newman (d. 1890), written in the year 1833, when he was still an Anglican. He recalls that Jesus said: Whoever wants to be his disciple must take up his cross "daily" (Lk 9:23). We know that this idea of a "daily duty" constitutes the cross. Normal crosses are the "everyday" ones. There are also great crosses, which, so to speak, befall us, and usually we also receive great strength to bear these great crosses. But the everyday crosses are the big challenge for the practice of self-denial.

Blessed John Henry Newman points out that taking up one's cross "daily" is still not enough. He says:

> It is right then almost to *find out* for yourself daily self-denials.... Determine to yield to others in things indifferent, to go out of your way in small matters, to inconvenience yourself (so that no direct duty suffers by it), rather than you should not meet with your daily discipline.

Newman uses a word here that has almost completely disappeared from our preaching and our everyday Christian vocabulary: the word "self-denial". He means it quite simply, in everyday things: "Let your very rising from your bed be a self-denial; let your meals be self-denials." And in this connection he cites Paul, who said about himself: "I pommel my body and subdue it, lest after preaching to others I myself should be disqualified" (1 Cor 9:27).

Newman is sober enough to know that

> this is a hard doctrine; hard to those even who assent to it, and can describe it most accurately. There are such imperfections, such inconsistencies in the heart and life of even

the better sort of men, that continual repentance must ever
go hand in hand with our endeavours to obey. Much we
need the grace of Christ's blood to wash us from the guilt
we daily incur.[13]

We know that the proof of following the way of the cross
is in little everyday things. "Friends of Christ's Cross" are
required not only to overcome their own self-centeredness
but also and above all to have positively the mind that was
in Christ. Saint Thomas Aquinas suggests that this depends
not so much on the difficulty of the sacrifice as on the
greatness of one's love. "[He] loved me and gave himself
for me" (Gal 2:20). What redeemed us was not the blood-
stained Cross, not the horrific sufferings of Jesus on the
Cross, but rather love, the love that lasts to the end.[14]

> For the love of Christ urges us on, because we are
> convinced that one has died for all; therefore all have died.
> And he died for all, that those who live might live no
> longer for themselves but for him who for their sake died
> and was raised. (2 Cor 5:14–15)

Following the way of the cross is nothing other than being
seized by the love of Christ. Along this way there are
experiences that are like turning points, where before and
after make a difference, points at which one's life with
Christ and for Christ acquires an entirely new dimension.
This very often has to do with concrete experiences of the
cross. Blessed Teresa of Calcutta (d. 1997) recalls one such
turning point in her life. She once said to her sisters:

[13] John Henry Newman, sermon 5, "Self-Denial the Test of Religious Earnest-
ness", in *Parochial and Plain Sermons* (San Francisco: Ignatius Press, 1997), 41–49.
[14] Cf. Thomas Aquinas, *Summa theologiae* III, 49.

When [your] Mother [Foundress] first picked up that woman who was eaten up by rats—her face, legs, and so on—if I had just passed by when I had seen and smelt her, I could not have been an MC [a Missionary of Charity]. But I returned, picked her up and took her to Campbell Hospital. If I had not, the Society would have died. Feelings of repugnance are human and if in spite of it we still give all our wholehearted free service, then we are on the right path and will be a holy sister.[15]

Following the way of the cross can occur at such turning points if we recognize Christ in the destitute. Seeing Christ in the poorest of the poor made Mother Teresa the foundress of her community. She liked to tell about an example from the life of Saint Elizabeth of Thüringen (d. 1231):

One day Queen Elizabeth offered hospitality to a leper man and even gave him her husband's bed to lie on. The mother-in-law, seeing this, seized the opportunity to set her son against his wife. The husband dashed angrily into the room, but to his surprise he saw the figure of Christ on the bed. Elizabeth could have acted thus only because she was convinced she was doing it to Christ Himself.[16]

This experience is not foreign to me, although I myself am a long way from really living it out profoundly. I am acquainted with individuals who live it out today credibly, people who encounter Christ in the destitute.

[15] Mother Teresa of Calcutta, *Where There Is Love, There Is God* (New York: Doubleday, 2010), 275.
[16] Ibid., 158.

Affliction and Suffering

We can love the cross only if we love our crucified Lord, which always means the Risen Lord, too, who even as the Risen One still has his wounds and remains the One who delivered himself up for us. But what do we do about the unspeakable, distressing suffering that we can encounter in this world? This suffering sometimes seems so great that the thought of it is stupefying. Some time ago I read a detailed article about the practice of torture worldwide and was aghast. We know about it, yet we do not think about it. The kinds of torture that occur today, at this hour, are unimaginable! Often at night I think about the prisons. Recently I read a report surveying the situation in prisons in most parts of the world. Whenever this passage from the Psalms is read in the Divine Office, "the LORD hears the cry of the imprisoned" (cf. Ps 69:33), I have to think about this reality in our world today, the unimaginable amount of wretchedness in the prisons of this world. We think about the human trafficking, right in front of our eyes here in Vienna, without our noticing it. How much misery due to sexual exploitation, violence, and fear. That is the cross, undiluted, in the cruelty with which it was originally invented, in order to put people to death. What do we say about this massive suffering, this inhumanity, in light of the cross? Is not all our talk about love for the cross and for the Crucified sheer helplessness in contrast?

I remember my first oral report in the fourth class in secondary school. I spoke about Henri Dunant (d. 1910), the founder of the Red Cross. How much was changed through the initiative of this one man, under the banner of the cross, even though it is secular and not necessarily to be viewed as the Christian cross. How many selfless, unconditional relief efforts worldwide, how much reparation for terrible losses has been done under the sign of the cross! In countless humanitarian aid initiatives the Cross of Christ continues to have its effect, even though it is not mentioned explicitly. It is the hidden, real source of selfless, dedicated assistance. Here the Crucified One is truly at work.

Given all this misery, the Cross of Christ is a refuge. We should take refuge often at the Cross of Christ and offer up to the Crucified and Risen One the whole cross of human suffering. It is important to say yes to the cross that is allotted to us and, in our suffering, in fear and helplessness, and in the midst of excessive demands, to embrace the cross, and this always means pressing the Crucified One to our heart. How many dying persons have had experiences of consolation and healing! One example would be the marvelous passage in the autobiography of the Little Flower, Saint Thérèse, about the murderer Pranzini, for whom she had prayed fervently as a fourteen-year-old. Shortly before his execution at the guillotine—he had rejected all religious assistance—he suddenly turned around, grabbed the crucifix that the priest was holding out to him, kissed it three times ardently, and then went to his death.

My father, shortly before his death, said something to me that I will never forget: "I read a sentence that deeply impressed me. It said: The front of the cross is suffering and death. The back is resurrection and joy."

VII

"Go into All the World"

Pupils Become Teachers

How do pupils become teachers? How do those whom Jesus has admitted to his school become persons whom he can send out as missionaries, as his witnesses? The Risen Lord summoned the apostles to the mount of the Beatitudes. There he appeared to them. Saint Matthew relates that the apostles fell down before him in awe and adoration, although some still had doubts. Then Jesus said to them:

> All authority in heaven and on earth has been given to me. Go therefore and make disciples of all nations, baptizing them in the name of the Father and of the Son and of the Holy Spirit, teaching them to observe all that I have commanded you. (Mt 28:18–20)

The Whole Teaching of Jesus

Pupils are there to learn something. The teacher's job is to make new pupils who can then teach. Jesus' disciples are also supposed to teach those whom they have made to be pupils of Jesus. Everything that they heard from their teacher, they are to hand on to them. This is how

Paul understands his task when he says: "I received from the Lord what I also delivered to you" (1 Cor 11:23). They are not supposed to hand on a little bit, piecemeal, but everything. "All that I have commanded you" (Mt 28:20) you should teach the others who through you become my disciples. But what is this "all"? Is it written anywhere? Where do the apostles, the disciples find all this? The pupils who have become teachers are supposed to hand on the Master's entire teaching. But where is this teaching to be found? How can you verify whether the teachers are really handing on the Lord's teaching or whether they are truncating it or mixing in something of their own, whether over the course of time, over the years and centuries, Jesus' teaching was changed and falsified? Since then two thousand years have passed. Has the teaching not long since become something different from what Jesus originally taught? The apostles were eyewitnesses who heard it themselves. He himself trained them, and they were his immediate personal disciples. As long as there were eyewitnesses who had heard the teaching firsthand, they could also check each other when they related what Jesus taught. They could exchange their recollections and verify whether they really handed on Jesus' teaching exactly. But after the death of the last apostle, who could guarantee that Jesus' teaching was not gradually being falsified? Over the course of the centuries have not many things accumulated that cover up and distort Jesus' teaching and make it unrecognizable? How do we know today what Jesus really taught, what his teaching originally was?

The *Catechism of the Catholic Church* is considered an authentic, valid summary of the Catholic doctrine of the faith today. But what things in the *Catechism* are really Jesus' teaching? Furthermore: Did Jesus have a teaching in the first place? Is there something like a clearly defined doctrine of Jesus that can be described? Are not the reports that we have about what Jesus taught and did always "filtered" through the lenses of the contemporary witnesses, through the lenses of their presuppositions, through their own notions that they brought with them, and through the way in which they adopted Jesus' words, deeds, and teachings, thus handing down their own view? We have only the four Gospels and the other New Testament writings. We cannot get to Jesus otherwise. But can we get past the New Testament authors and have direct access to Jesus? Or do we still have only what the witnesses reported from their perspective? These are questions with which anyone who deals with theology becomes familiar, and they pose many problems. Did John not draw a different picture of Jesus from the one in Matthew? And is Mark not quite different from Luke? Each one has his central idea, his own emphases. Is the Sermon on the Mount, as Matthew records it, really Jesus' teaching to which we should hold fast? Are the parables found only in Luke really Jesus' teaching or Luke's interpretation? And are the many discourses of Jesus recorded in the Gospel of John really Jesus' teaching, or are they not instead an exegesis by John the Theologian? In short: Do we find Jesus himself in the New Testament? Only then can we speak about a teaching of Jesus, about what he himself really said to his disciples, what he commanded them to teach.

This question preoccupied me as a young student, and again and again I notice that it also affects people who deal with theology today and often react with confusion.

Joseph Ratzinger, Pope Benedict XVI, has given us three volumes about *Jesus of Nazareth*. He dealt intensively with this question and thereby started a worldwide discussion: Can we trust the Gospels? Does the depiction of Jesus in the Gospels really show Jesus, or does it paint over the reality and give us an interpretation, just as there are many images of Jesus and all sorts of interpretations of Christ?

Benedict XVI did not neglect modern biblical scholarship; he knows it as well as almost anyone else among the great theologians of our time. Throughout his life he has studied the word of God, the Bible, intensively, especially the New Testament, and exegesis, biblical scholarship, too. He himself says that he intends, without neglecting modern exegesis, "to try to portray the Jesus of the Gospels as the real, 'historical' Jesus in the strict sense of the word." And he says: "I believe that this Jesus—the Jesus of the Gospels—is a historically plausible and convincing figure."[1] If we want to have sure access to Jesus' teaching, we can trust the Gospels. "Teach them to observe all that I have taught you." Everything that Jesus taught we find first in the Gospels.

Saint Thérèse of Lisieux died at the age of only twenty-four; she never held a professorial chair at a university, yet she is a Doctor of the Church. In her autobiographical manuscripts it says: "But above all it's the Gospels that occupy my mind when I'm at prayer; my poor soul has so many needs, and yet this is the one thing needful. I'm always finding fresh lights there, hidden and enthralling meanings."[2] Thérèse finds everything in the Gospel: "Teach them to observe all that I have taught you."

[1] Pope Benedict XVI/Joseph Ratzinger, *Jesus of Nazareth*, vol. 1, trans. Adrian J. Walker (New York: Doubleday, 2007), xxii.

[2] Thérèse of Lisieux, *ms autob*. A, 83v; cited in *CCC* 127.

Saint Jerome says: "Ignorance of the Scriptures is ignorance of Christ" (cited in *CCC* 133). It impresses me again
and again when I meet people who are "at home" in Sacred
Scripture, who have "devoured" the word of God, as the
Prophet Jeremiah once said: "Your words were found,
and I ate them" (cf. Jer 15:16). People who hunger and
thirst for the word of God, people who have the word of
God imprinted on their souls. It increasingly becomes the
word on which they live, the word that to some extent is
their subsistence.

The Power of the Proclamation

It must have been remarkable to experience Jesus as a
teacher: "When Jesus finished these sayings, the crowds
were astonished at his teaching, for he taught them as one
who had authority, and not as their scribes" (Mt 7:28–29).
His disciples seem to have acquired and radiated something of the power of his teaching. For after Easter and
Pentecost they appeared in public with great power
and authority. "Every day in the temple and at home they
did not cease teaching and preaching Jesus as the Christ"
(Acts 5:42). Again and again we find the expression *meta
paresias*, with confidence, with power, with authority.
Jesus' teaching lives on in the teaching of the apostles. It
has astonishing, surprising power; the Acts of the Apostles
as a whole testifies to this many times. For instance, there
was the healing of the crippled beggar at the golden or
"Beautiful Gate" of the Temple. As a result, Peter and
John were interrogated before the High Council, and we
read: "When they saw the boldness of Peter and John, and
perceived that they were uneducated, common men, they

wondered" (Acts 4:13). They marveled that they preached with such power and clarity.

The teaching of the apostles does not consist of cleverly devised theories but is powerful and clear. It has just one theme: Jesus Christ, the Lord. It is impossible for them to keep silent about him. They can no longer conceal his name; they must speak about him, although the High Council demands that they must never again preach and teach in the name of Jesus. People experienced them therefore as men who preach and teach the name of Jesus. The apostles reply: "We cannot but speak of what we have seen and heard" (Acts 4:20).

So it was back then at the beginning: they proclaimed and taught the person of Jesus Christ. That was the novelty, the essential content of their teaching. But did that continue to be the case?

Meanwhile, over the course of two thousand years, have not other teachings latched on to it and surrounded it, which make it much more difficult to say what is really Jesus' teaching and what was added later? Is everything taught by the Second Vatican Council and by the *Catechism* "Jesus' teaching"? Is it not much too complicated? Is Jesus not much simpler than that? Is all that still in keeping with the uneducated apostles who stood before the High Council? Do you have to have all this doctrinal gear in your backpack in order to be a Christian today?

We observe that knowledge of the doctrine of the faith is tragically lacking to a great extent among the people of God. Commentators speak today about the "illiteracy" of Christians in faith matters. With all those doctrines and the many thick books, where do we find the center of Christ's teaching, its living heart, so to speak? If it is not supposed to be a matter for scholars and specialists but precisely for simple people, then Jesus' teaching must also be accessible and within reach, understandable and practicable, especially for those to whom Jesus attributed in a particular way the knowledge of his teaching. "I thank you, Father, Lord of heaven and earth, that you have hidden these things from the wise and understanding and revealed them to infants" (Mt 11:25).

Simple Faith

In his exegesis of the closing words of the Gospel of Matthew, Saint John Chrysostom notes that Jesus' command, "[Teach] them to observe all that I have commanded you", comes immediately after the command to baptize: "Go ... and make disciples of all nations, baptizing them in the name of the Father and of the Son and of the Holy Spirit." "Jesus commands them to pour out over the whole world the doctrine about baptism that he entrusted to them as a summary of all his teaching."[3]

Chrysostom sees Jesus' teaching as his teaching about baptism; baptismal catechesis is the summa of Jesus' teaching. It is no accident that the ancient Church regarded the catechumenate, the preparation of adults for baptism, as especially important and indispensable. In the catechumenate, Jesus' teaching is instilled in them. Above all, it should be received interiorly.

Often in my experience I have found in very simple people an especially deep knowledge of Jesus' teaching. Again and again I have pondered the question: Where

[3] Saint John Chrysostom, hom. 90–91 on the Gospel of Matthew, trans. from: *Homilien über das Evangelium des hl. Matthäus*, trans. Prinz Max von Sachsen (Regensburg, 1911), 615.

do they get this knowledge? Where does this deep understanding, this unshakable clarity about the Lord and about his doctrine come from? I found an intellectual starting point for this rock-solid certainty of mine many years ago in a homily by Cardinal Ratzinger that he gave as Archbishop of Munich on New Year's Eve, December 31, 1979, at the cathedral in Munich. He starts with baptism.[4]

In the news at that time was the withdrawal of the license to teach from Professor Hans Küng, the Swiss theologian, a professor in Tübingen and a colleague of Professor Ratzinger. The withdrawal of the *missio canonica*, that is, of permission to teach in the name of the Catholic Church, Cardinal Ratzinger recalls, was widely stigmatized as authoritarian suppression, as an attack on the sacred and fundamental right of freedom of inquiry. In Switzerland a heated debate was being conducted at the time. Freedom to express one's opinion seemed to have been banned from the Church, and human rights were somehow being trampled underfoot. This discussion revolved especially around the question of professing Christ. The debate then came to a head with the question: Are there any obligatory formulas of faith in the first place? Can the faith be grasped in formulas at all? Can Jesus' teaching, can what pertains to the person of Jesus, be reduced to concepts or doctrinal propositions? If so, what statements fit Jesus? Do these statements always fit, even today, or only back then in particular times and cultures?

---

[4] "Was ihr von Anfang an gehört habt, soll in euch bleiben". Homily, December 31, 1979. Munich: Pressereferat der Erzdiözese München-Freising [Press Office of the Archdiocese of Munich and Freising], 1980. Reprinted in the German weekly edition of *L'Osservatore Romano*.

In his New Year's Eve homily, Cardinal Ratzinger says:

> The Christian faith ... appeared from the beginning in formulas: I think that this is consequently the case for us. Paul pointed this out so clearly in chapter 6 of the Letter to the Romans. In verse 17 Paul makes a statement that is of the utmost importance for us: "Thanks be to God, that you who were once slaves of sin have become obedient from the heart to the standard [*typos*] of teaching to which you were committed."

This is a literal rendering of a rather strange, difficult formula.

Paul is addressing the topic of obedience: You have become obedient from the heart to the teaching. Ratzinger says: "For Paul, the opposite of slavery or lack of freedom is not the complete absence of limitations or commitments, but rather obedience that comes from the heart." "Obedience from the heart" is not servile submission but, rather, loving compliance with the will of another in trust, in freedom. Jesus lived in obedience to his Father, in complete trust, in freedom, in compliance with his will. Disobedience to the will of God was precisely the cause of our loss of freedom. Obedience to God's will is freedom. Jesus' pupils, his disciples, can become teachers of the faith themselves only if they are "obedient from the heart", listening to the will and the word of God.

Cardinal Ratzinger continues:

> But now there is another very important point: Obedience has a very specific content: Paul relates it to the "*typos* of teaching to which you were committed". Here the apostle is referring ... to the profession of faith [the Creed] or else

to a catechetical formulation of the teaching that is the content of baptism.

Baptism is not just any ritual but, rather, "an essential procedure". It is entrance into a common form, into the common profession of faith, into the faith of the Church. The faith includes very concrete articles or "statements of content that are understandable for everyone". Cardinal Ratzinger explains the articles of the faith by means of a helpful distinction. He says that the articles of the faith are "inexhaustible" but "not incomprehensible and arbitrary". They are inexhaustible "and therefore can always be studied in greater depth", but not indeterminate, so that everyone could make whatever he wanted out of them. Faith that Jesus is the Christ, the Son of the living God, is something quite definite, even if it is inexhaustible. Paul is saying something peculiar: "Tradition is not committed to the newly baptized person, but rather the newly baptized person is committed to the tradition. It does not become his property, which he can shape arbitrarily, but rather he becomes its property. It is the larger form that shapes him, and not the other way around." Paul is saying: "You were committed to the *typos* of the teaching." We are not owners of the faith, but, rather, we are handed over to the faith. Just as a disciple can become Jesus' pupil only if he hands himself over and entrusts himself to the Master completely and allows him to form him, so, too, he certainly cannot be a teacher if he has not completely committed himself to the teaching of Jesus. Jesus' teaching is the standard, the guideline, the *canon* of teaching.

I would like to add some personal testimony, In Fribourg we had a charismatic prayer group. The charismatic renewal was still very young. In this prayer group, I, a priest and a university professor, was a "simple member". It was headed by a man, François Baetig, who was a gardener. He was a genuine teacher to me in matters concerning Jesus, not only because of his sober, deep piety, but also because of his very sure sense of what the faith teaches and what is not part of the faith. He did not get this sense from a course of study at the university, but, rather, he possessed an interior knowledge that resulted from long experience of the faith, from a deep prayer life, from a firsthand familiarity with the Lord. When François spoke about the Eucharist, I knew that he was speaking about reality. When I gave lectures about the Eucharist, there was a lot of knowledge in them, many things that were historical, theological, and the fruit of reflection, but it was always clear to me that François, the leader of our prayer group, knew what he was talking about when he spoke about the Eucharist. For him it was not learned theory but, rather, experiential knowledge. Of course he knew his catechism, young people still learned it back then. (It is one of the great misfortunes of recent generations that we no longer know the basics. In many meetings with Muslims I think of how precisely they can recite their "catechism", which is certainly learned by rote, but they do know it. Members of our younger generation never acquired this support structure, and consequently they find it difficult to say what the real core of Christ's teaching is, what it consists of and what it means when expressed in concrete formulas.) With our gardener François, though, it was not just book knowledge from the catechism. I have often reflected on it theologically as well: What was it actually? In this reflection the New Year's Eve homily of Cardinal

Ratzinger was a "key experience" for me. In his contro-
versy with Hans Küng, the Archbishop of Munich referred
to the reading for the day, December 31, from the First
Letter of John. There it says:

> You have been anointed by the Holy One, and you all
> know.... Any one who denies the Son does not have the
> Father. He who confesses the Son has the Father also. Let
> what you heard from the beginning abide in you. If what
> you heard from the beginning abides in you, then you will
> abide in the Son and in the Father.... I write this to you
> about those who would deceive you; but the anointing
> which you received from him abides in you, and you have
> no need that any one should teach you; as his anointing
> teaches you about everything, and is true, and is no lie, just
> as it has taught you, abide in him. (1 Jn 2:20–27)

Cardinal Ratzinger explains the concrete situation that
the apostle John has in mind in this letter: Gnosticism.
This teaching, which was then coming into fashion, tried
to interpret Christianity symbolically for people who had
more education. Divine Sonship, virginal conception, resurrection, the empty tomb: all of that was merely symbolic;
Jesus' miracles: nothing but symbolism. For the "finer
minds", the more educated people, you would not want
something so crude and literal as the faith of the "primitive
people"; rather, you would want a Christianity that was
in keeping with the mind-set of the time. Is Christianity, is the teaching of Jesus, something literal for "primitive" souls and something symbolic for the "more clever",
the educated? Are simple believers primitive when they
believe that Jesus' miracles really happened that way, that

he really was conceived by the Virgin Mary through the Holy Spirit, that he really rose from the dead, just as the Gospel tells us?

John defends the faith of the "simple faithful": "You have been anointed, and you all know.... You know the truth.... The anointing which you received from him abides in you, and you have no need that any one should teach you." Ratzinger explains: By "anointing", John means in the first place Christ himself: "You have Christ, the 'Anointed One', and you do not need to have someone teach you." He himself teaches us everything. Having him, knowing him, loving him is the way to know his teaching. He is that teaching "in person". The word "anointing" refers also, though, to "baptism and to the common faith transmitted in baptism".

> What John writes here could therefore be reduced to the formula: Learned men do not determine what is true in the baptismal faith, but rather the baptismal faith determines what is valid in learned exegeses. The intellectuals do not measure the simple, but rather the simple measure the intellectuals. Intellectual interpretations are not the standard for the baptismal profession of faith, but rather the baptismal profession in its naïve literalness is the standard for all theology. A baptized person who abides in his baptismal faith needs no instruction. He has received the decisive truth and carries it within him with the faith itself.

These words of Cardinal Ratzinger were for me at the beginning of the new year 1980 the intellectual confirmation of what I as a young professor was experiencing vividly with the leader of our prayer group. When he, a simple gardener, spoke about faith matters, I could tell that this clear faith always had to be the standard for my work as a teacher of theology. I must never claim, as a "learned theologian", to be above the faith of simple believers. My job as a professor of theology was to serve that faith, to show the beauty and consistency of it, and to defend it against attacks.

Cardinal Ratzinger, who at that time was not yet Prefect of the Congregation for the Doctrine of the Faith, summed up the task of the Church's teaching authority as follows: "The Church's Magisterium protects the faith of simple believers; of those who do not write books, do not talk on television, and cannot write newspaper editorials: That is its democratic task. It is supposed to give a voice to those who have none."

I had the privilege of doing this again and again during my work as a theology professor: being a voice for the simple believers. Demonstrating the coherence of the Church's doctrine of the faith and hearing in it the living teaching of Jesus, through study, research, working with the great masters of theology, the Church Fathers, Saint Thomas Aquinas, and the men and women doctors of the Church.

Let us return to the question with which we started: How do the disciples, Jesus' pupils, become teachers of the faith? One initial thing has become clear: the genuine teachers of the faith always remain in the Master's school, remain disciples of the Lord. We have never completely learned what it means to follow him. Life with Jesus, intimate converse with him, is still the source from which all teaching flows. This is true for parents who want to

pass their faith on to their children; it is true for the theology professor who reflects on the faith. This is my own
experience from sixteen years of teaching: however indispensable, thorough, and diligent study may be, the really
deep insights come from converse with the Lord, when in
meditation or in prayer "a light goes on" and something
is grasped from within. This, then, is "the anointing that
teaches us about everything", as John says.

A second point became clear: part of being a Christian teacher of the faith is knowledge, to put it simply,
familiarity with Sacred Scripture, especially the Gospels.
But also that fundamental knowledge of the faith that Paul
called the "*typos* of teaching", which is summarized in the
Creed. It is not primarily a collection of propositions but,
rather, consists of events and facts: that God really is the
Creator of all things, that Jesus really is the Christ, the
Son of the living God, was really conceived by the Virgin Mary, really became man for us and for our salvation,
really suffered, died, and was buried and truly arose, and
that the Holy Spirit really upholds the one, holy, catholic,
and apostolic Church.

The teaching that the disciples are supposed to hand on
is above all the acknowledgment of these facts. Of what
else does the teaching of Saint Paul consist, then? He himself says it quite clearly:

> For I delivered to you as of first importance what I also
> received, that Christ died for our sins in accordance with
> the Scriptures, that he was buried, that he was raised
> on the third day in accordance with the Scriptures, and
> that he appeared to Cephas, then to the Twelve.... So we
> preach and so you believed. (1 Cor 15:3–5, 11)

Teachers Are Witnesses

The Risen Lord said to his disciples who were gathered in the Cenacle:

> "Thus it is written, that the Christ should suffer and on the third day rise from the dead, and that repentance and forgiveness of sins should be preached in his name to all nations, beginning from Jerusalem. You are witnesses of these things. And behold, I send the promise of my Father upon you." (Lk 24:46–49)

Teachers should not only teach but be witnesses. As Pope Paul VI (d. 1978) famously put it: "Modern man listens more willingly to witnesses than to teachers, and if he does listen to teachers, it is because they are witnesses."[5] This oft-quoted remark is a true echo of what Jesus said to his disciples: "You shall be my witnesses" (Acts 1:8).

Witness in Greek is *martys*. A witness is a martyr. Pupils become teachers by becoming witnesses. When we look at martyrs, it becomes clear that the teaching that Jesus entrusts to his disciples is above all a profession, a testimony. "Every one who acknowledges me before men, I also will acknowledge before my Father who is in heaven" (Mt 10:32). The proclamation of the Gospel is not possible without enmity and persecution. Erik Peterson (d. 1960) says in his famous tract *Witness to the Truth* (*Zeuge der Wahrheit*, 1937, written right in the middle of the Nazi era): "As long as the Gospel is preached in this

---

[5] Paul VI, Apostolic Exhortation *Evangelii nuntiandi* (December 8, 1975), 41.

world—and so until the end of time—the Church will have martyrs, too."[6]

Even though not all Christians are called to martyrdom, they are called to witness, and part of that is the cross. Taking it up daily is the way to follow Christ. But Jesus' commission: "[Teach] them to observe all that I have commanded you" is followed by the steadfast promise: "Behold, I am with you always, to the close of the age" (Mt 28:20).

[6] Erik Peterson, *Zeuge der Wahrheit*, 176; Peterson, *Ausgewählte Schriften*, vol. 1 (Würzburg, 1994), 100.

VIII

"Where Two or Three Are Gathered in My Name"

The Holy Spirit as Interior Teacher

In his farewell discourse, which he held in the Cenacle on the night before his Passion, Jesus says: "But the Counselor, the Holy Spirit, whom the Father will send in my name, he will teach you all things, and bring to your remembrance all that I have said to you" (Jn 14:26). Jesus promised and sent the Holy Spirit, the *Parakletos*. The term *parakletos* can be translated as counselor, intercessor, advocate, but also consoler. Jesus commissioned the apostles to make disciples or pupils of all nations and to teach them to follow everything "that I have commanded you" (Mt 28:20).

This is precisely what the Holy Spirit does—what the apostles and the Holy Spirit do, we and the Holy Spirit. The Holy Spirit will teach everything. He will remind us of everything. They can teach *all* that Jesus commanded them when the Holy Spirit has taught them everything. For how are we supposed to teach all that Jesus commanded us if we do not know it all? Is it not odd that we encounter *all* in the Bible so often, even on the first page?

It would be worthwhile to read through the whole Bible looking for the word "all" or "everything". "And God saw *everything* that he had made, and behold, it was very good", we read at the conclusion of the Creation account (Gen 1:31). And at the very end of the Bible, in the Book of Revelation, we read again: "Behold, I make *all things* new" (Rev 21:5).

The Spirit as Helper

Do we really know it "all"? Jesus communicated everything to us, but did it all sink in? Did we perhaps not understand everything that Jesus commanded us? But you can only teach what you know and, above all, what you understand. If the teacher does not understand what he teaches, should he really be teaching, then? But who among us already knows it all? Much less already understands it all? Are we not rather in the situation that Paul describes: "Our knowledge is imperfect.... For now we see in a mirror dimly, but then face to face. Now I know in part; then I shall understand fully, even as I have been fully understood" (1 Cor 13:9, 12)? He distinguishes between now and then: "Now we walk by faith, then we will walk by sight"; now our understanding is fragmentary, then we will see him as he is and will understand everything.

Pope Benedict XVI said this impressively at the meeting of religions in Assisi, to which he invited several agnostics, too. He spoke about the fact that all of us of course are pilgrims on the way to truth. As pilgrims who are on the way, how are we supposed to "teach all that Jesus commanded us"? The tension is painful. On the one hand, we believe that the whole truth is entrusted to us, not just little bits and pieces. There is no secret revelation for a select few, who then know a little more, whereas the others know less. Jesus says: "All that I have heard from my Father I have made known to you" [Jn 15:15]. Paul says in the Letter to the Romans: "He who did not spare his own Son but gave him up for us all, will he not also give us all things with him?" (Rom 8:32). Therefore we have received it all, but do we possess it all yet? Has it taken hold of us to the point where we are completely seized and gripped by it? Did not Jesus himself tell us that we still have a way ahead of us? We have received everything, but we do not understand it all. He says explicitly in his farewell discourse: "I have yet many things to say to you, but you cannot bear them now" (Jn 16:12). He then goes on to say: "When the Spirit of truth comes, he will guide you into all the truth", literally: "lead you on the path to all truth". This can be translated verbatim: He will give you "guidance on the way to all truth". Therefore, Jesus himself says that the truth has been given, but we cannot yet comprehend it fully. We cannot yet bear it in its entirety; we must still be led into it. For this purpose, he sent the Holy Spirit.

The truth is not a theory but a person. To the apostle Thomas, Jesus said: "I am the way, and the truth, and the life" (Jn 14:6). But we need a guide, we need someone who takes us by the hand and leads us. For we are pilgrims, seekers, we are on a journey. We walk the path of faith. The Council reminds us that even Mary, the Mother of God, walked the path of faith. And Pope John Paul II adds that she went through "the night of faith". We understand only imperfectly, but we are not left alone on this path.

"I will not leave you desolate", Jesus says; "I will come to you" (Jn 14:18). He says this, not primarily about his final return, when he comes back in heavenly glory with his angels at the Last Judgment at the end of the ages, nor primarily about the end of our life, when we encounter him as our judge and redeemer at the personal judgment. I already come to you now. Even now he keeps his promise: "I am with you always" (Mt 28:20). It does not say: I will be with you, but, rather: I am with you!

But how does this happen? How do we experience this? What does the working of the Holy Spirit look like? How does the Holy Spirit teach us everything, as Jesus promised? Saint Augustine elaborated on this in his doctrine about the *magister interior*, the "interior teacher". The Holy Spirit is the one who teaches us, not from outside, as human teachers do, but from within. Let us recall our own experience of this. How do we experience the teaching of the Holy Spirit? In Jesus' farewell discourse in the Cenacle, he mentions three particular ways in which the Holy Spirit works. These three sayings of Jesus indicate the program, so to speak, for the working of the Holy Spirit.

1. "He will ... bring to your remembrance all that I have said to you" (Jn 14:26). The Holy Spirit reminds us.

2. "But when the Counselor comes, whom I shall send to you from the Father, even the Spirit of truth, who proceeds from the Father, he will bear witness to me; and you also are witnesses, because you have been with me from the beginning" (Jn 15:26). The Holy Spirit gives witness, just as we should, may, and can give witness. The Holy Spirit makes us aware of Jesus, brings him close to us. Behind this idea is the Greek word "martyrdom", *martyresei*; he will be a witness to Jesus.

3. "When [the Paraclete, the Counselor] comes, he will convince the world of sin and of righteousness and of judgment" (Jn 16:8). The Holy Spirit convicts sin.

In his testament in the farewell discourse on the night before his Passion, the Lord committed to his disciples three activities of the Holy Spirit: reminding, witnessing, and convicting.

Remembrance of God's Deeds

The *Catechism* says: "The Holy Spirit is the Church's living memory" (*CCC* 1099). Although we often get the impression that the Church is distracted, that we are or I am distracted, we can rely on the fact that the Holy Spirit reminds us. The whole Bible is full of the theme of remembering. The Jewish tradition to this day is above all a tradition of bearing in mind, or remembrance. "Do not forget the works of God." It is like a refrain through the whole Bible: Remember, Israel! Forget not! The Holy Spirit is, so to speak, the one who prompts us, so that we do not become forgetful but remember.

This occurs, for instance, in the anamnesis of the Mass, where after the words of consecration we are reminded of God's works. The *Catechism* comments: "The liturgical celebration always refers to God's saving interventions in history" (*CCC* 1103). Creation, the election of the People of God with Abraham, the Exodus from Egypt, the Temple, and the Exile are works of God. "The economy of Revelation is realized by deeds and words which are intrinsically bound up with each other.... [T]he words ... proclaim the works and bring to light the mystery they contain" (*Dei*

Verbum, 2, as quoted in *CCC* 1103). Words and deeds are always connected with each other in the Bible and shed light on each other. In the Liturgy of the Word, the Holy Spirit reminds the congregation of all that Christ did for us, most solemnly at the Easter Vigil with the nine readings, which go through the whole great history of the People of God, from Creation to the Paschal Mystery. In keeping with the nature of the liturgical actions and the traditional rites of the Church, a liturgical celebration recalls the great deeds of God in a more or less detailed anamnesis. The Holy Spirit, who thus awakens the memory of the Church, incites thanksgiving and praise. From remembrance follows doxology, singing the praise of God.

The Eucharist is a great remembrance, commemoration. We commemorate in every Mass the death and Resurrection of Jesus Christ. But what sort of commemoration or remembrance is it?

> In the sense of Sacred Scripture the *memorial* is not merely the recollection of past events but the proclamation of the mighty works wrought by God for men. In the liturgical celebration of these events, they become in a certain way present and real. This is how Israel understands its liberation from Egypt: every time Passover is celebrated, the Exodus events are made present to the memory of believers so that they may conform their lives to them. (*CCC* 1363)

Everyone who participates in the Paschal meal, in the Seder, so the Jewish tradition says, should regard himself as someone who is now setting out from Egypt. We are contemporaries with the event that we remember, which thereby becomes present. We are contemporaries with the

apostles in the Cenacle, when the priest speaks the words
that Jesus spoke in the Cenacle. We remember, and at the
same time they are present. At Christmas we take it for
granted that we should sing: "Today our Savior is born",
even though it was two thousand years ago. It is now! In
our remembrance, it is the present, and so it is too with
the Paschal event: Christ is risen today! In this recollec-
tion, in this remembering, the Holy Spirit makes present
what happened once at that time, but once and for all. It
becomes present when we remember it. Nowhere is that
so clear as in the Eucharist.

> In the New Testament, the memorial takes on new
> meaning. When the Church celebrates the Eucharist, she
> commemorates Christ's Passover, and it is made present:
> the sacrifice Christ offered once for all on the cross remains
> ever present. "As often as the sacrifice of the Cross by
> which 'Christ our Pasch has been sacrificed' is celebrated
> on the altar, the work of our redemption is carried out."
> (*CCC* 1364, citing *Lumen gentium* 3 and 1 Cor 5:7)

This happens today, if we celebrate it in remembrance.
The Holy Spirit reminds us and thereby makes it present. This is true of all the sacraments: when we admin-
ister baptism, Christ is the one who baptizes; when we
give absolution in confession, Christ, now present, is the
one who gives absolution. But we are always remembering
what Christ instituted, what he once did. By the action
of the Holy Spirit, Christ acts now. What is true for the
liturgy is true also for our own life. The Holy Spirit helps
us to remember what the Lord is accomplishing in our life.

I would like to illustrate various dimensions of this. One
is the experience of Sacred Scripture, the fact that Christ

often speaks to us quite personally through his word, through the word of the Gospel. I have often found that a Gospel reading, a passage from the Old Testament, or one from the New Testament letters very suddenly reveals a new dimension. It tells me something that I had previously not noticed at all. It is always an enlivening of the Lord's presence. The joy, but also the bewilderment over such a remembrance prompted by the Holy Spirit, is something very special. It is as though the Holy Spirit were speaking Jesus' words now for me personally.

One summer I was helping out at a small parish in the Swiss mountains. One morning at Mass I read the Gospel of the day, about the "miraculous multiplication of the loaves", which I had read many times before. Jesus had spent an entire day taking care of a gigantic crowd of people, healing many who were sick, teaching them at length, and then, when evening fell, his disciples came to him and said: "This is a lonely place, and the day is now over; send the crowds away to go into the villages and buy food for themselves" (Mt 14:15). Suddenly, the words "send the crowds away" struck me very personally. I was truly alarmed. Since that experience, even though it is thirty years ago now, I cannot hear this Gospel passage without being deeply moved. Suddenly the whole import of this saying was before me, the distressing fact of their all-too-human lack of understanding for Jesus. It is quite understandable that the disciples were tired in the evening and wanted the people to go away at last so that they themselves could finally have something to eat, and that is why they said: Send the people away, so that we can have a little rest. But these words struck me: "Send the crowds away."

Another example: When Jesus once saw a man with a withered hand in the synagogue, he placed him in the middle and asked those present: " 'Is it lawful on the sabbath to do good or to do harm, to save life or to kill?' But they were silent." Mark says: "And he looked around at them with anger, grieved at their hardness of heart." After he healed the man, "the Pharisees went out, and immediately held counsel with the Herodians against him, how to destroy him" (Mk 3:1–6). What a sorrow that must have been for Jesus, their hardness of heart! What must he have felt! I think that this, too, is a reminder of the Holy Spirit: when sometimes it is granted to us to glimpse what took place in the divine-human heart of Jesus. In this way I begin to see what it may mean to share Jesus' sufferings and therefore to experience the fervent desire, which we read about so often in the lives of the saints, to share in Jesus' sufferings or at least not to increase them through my own hard-heartedness. We should immediately add that this sorrow of Jesus, on which many saints have meditated so intensely, is inseparably connected with an incomparable joy of Jesus. This, too, is a gift of the Holy Spirit; it is possible to sense this, too. What a joy it must have been when Jesus said about the pagan centurion: "Not even in Israel have I found such faith" (Lk 7:9). To the pagan woman from the region of Sidon and Tyre, he says: "O woman, great is your faith" (Mt 15:28). Sensing and savoring Jesus' joy when he meets such people is also an unmistakable work of the Holy Spirit. Jesus says: "Abide in my love.... These things I have spoken to you, that my joy may be in you, and that your joy may be full" (Jn 15:9–11).

Paul must have experienced something of this joy (just as he also knew Jesus' sorrow), if he mentions joy right after love as one of the fruits of the Spirit (Gal 5:22). The Spirit bestows joy. It must have been the same for Peter. He must have known something of this unmistakable taste of the joy of the Holy Spirit if he says in the First Letter of Peter:

> Without having seen him [Jesus Christ] you love him; though you do not now see him you believe in him and rejoice with unutterable and exalted joy. As the outcome of your faith you obtain the salvation of your souls. (1 Pet 1:8–9)

Obtaining a share in Jesus' life and, so to speak, being able to experience it with him from within, his sorrow, his joy: that is the work of the Holy Spirit. It is not the same sort of reminder as when my smartphone suddenly beeps and I am reminded of an appointment. It is an entirely different sort of reminder, an insight into the Lord. There are many testimonies to this experience in the history of Christian life. "You in me and I in you", it says often in the Gospel of John. "Christ in me", "Christ in us", we read again and again in the letters of Paul. Or very succinctly: "in Christ". The reminder of the Holy Spirit grants this gift: a consciousness of Christ.

I have noticed that people who are very closely united with Christ, who live "in Christ", often have a very good memory. That may also be a special gift. I am thinking of our Pope Benedict XVI, whom I have known for forty years. There are few human beings who have such a fantastic memory, a special gift. But there is something else that is different. It has to do with the fact that the Holy Spirit leads people who allow themselves to be filled with him and, thus, to live in union with the Lord, out of themselves, so to speak, so that they no longer revolve around themselves. They are not caught up in themselves and, therefore, perceive other people much more intensely and consequently remember much better, also. Again and again I am amazed at how people who have a lively faith, a close union with the Lord, are simply alert to other people. In the writings of Paul M. Zulehner I found a beautiful observation: "Someone who is immersed in God surfaces among human beings." That is an experience granted by the Holy Spirit, and it includes the simple things, the fact that a person remembers birthdays and anniversaries of deaths, wedding days, and all kinds of things, people's names and what interests them, what they have suffered and what sort of aspirations they have. All this, too, is a part of this wonderful reminding by the Holy Spirit.

The Spirit Gives Witness to Christ

The Holy Spirit gives witness to Christ. He makes us his witnesses. In order for us to be able to be Christ's witnesses, the witness of the Holy Spirit is necessary. At an early age I found it fascinating to get to know people who were taught interiorly by the Holy Spirit, who are witnesses, not through their studies, but through this interior knowledge. "He will teach you all things", Jesus says. That does not mean that the Holy Spirit will teach us all technologies, for instance, how to use the computer, or everything that can be learned; rather, he will teach us the essential things: everything that is helpful and leads to an orientation in life. The Holy Spirit teaches all this. He accomplishes this interiorly through his seven gifts.

I could tell stories about many people who gave me the strong impression that they have an interior teacher. They know these things, not from books, but from an interior sense. I told you about François Baetig, the leader of our prayer group. He was such a person. I encountered another one very early on, and since then he has not let go of me: first his writings, then his life story, and finally his widow, Franziska. I mean Blessed Franz Jägerstätter (d. 1943), whom I discovered as a twenty-two-year-old student through the book by Gordon Zahn, *Er folgte seinem Gewissen* [He followed his conscience] (Graz, 1967). From the very beginning, he fascinated me by the clarity of his judgment, by the penetrating intellectual power of this simple farmer, who had only an elementary school education. He was certainly a gifted, intelligent man, but the clarity of his faith was the primary source of his gift of discernment, which he had to a degree that many university professors in the Nazi era did not have.

We can only marvel at the sureness with which this simple man grasped the intellectual and political situation of his time, how he distinguished lies from truth, how he chose a lonely path of refusing to serve Hitler in the military, even though he met with no understanding from parish priests or his bishop. Yet he always refrained from judging others who did not take his path. He always said, "I have received the grace for it. That is why I must follow this path." The exciting thing about Jägerstätter for me is that through the witness of this Spirit-led individual, it has also become possible to discern the signs of the times. Since the Council, we have talked a lot about the signs of the times. But how does one recognize them? Not from statistics and not from newspaper headlines. The martyrs, the witnesses to the faith, show where the wounds and the essential points of a particular time are. Franz Jägerstätter's lonely witness correctly showed the way to all of Austria, even though only a few in our country were able to follow it as he did. Above all Jägerstätter—and this is the power of witnesses—discerned where the demonic was ultimately at work in the National Socialist ideology. He clearly recognized what was at stake here. That is the martyr's task: to draw our attention to what matters.

He says: "All the same, I think that the Lord God is making it not that difficult for us now to lay down our lives for our faith. For if you reflect that in these difficult times of war thousands of young men have already been called on to lay down their lives for National Socialism, and many have had to sacrifice their lives in this fight [*Kampf*]: Why then should it be harder to lay down your life for a King who does not just impose duties on us, but also gives us rights, whose final victory is certain and whose kingdom, for which we thereby fight, will last forever?" Not just the supposed thousand years of Hitler's *Reich*.

The Holy Spirit Convicts and Convinces

Thirdly and finally, perhaps the most difficult point: The Holy Spirit, Jesus says, "will convince the world of sin and of righteousness and of judgment: of sin, because they do not believe in me; of righteousness, because I go to the Father, and you will see me no more; of judgment, because the ruler of this world is judged" (Jn 16:8–11). Is

the Holy Spirit like an investigative journalist or a whistle-
blower? Is that not a rather strange perspective? Does the
Holy Spirit, who will teach us everything, expose injustice
relentlessly? He is the Spirit of truth, but is the truth a process of convicting and convincing? Where, then, is love? I
remember a dinner with Blessed Pope John Paul II. Back
then in the 1980s I was a young theologian, just appointed
to the International Theological Commission. The Holy
Father had invited the theologians to the midday meal.
Right beside the Pope sat Hans Urs von Balthasar (d. 1988),
the great Swiss theologian. I listened to how they talked
together about the meaning of the verse: "The Spirit will
convict/convince the world." We were able to read the
pope's meditations on this shortly afterward in his wonderful encyclical on the Holy Spirit (*Dominum et vivificantem*).
The pope meditates first on Pentecost and shows how the
Holy Spirit then "convinces the world of sin":

> Beginning from this initial witness at Pentecost and for all
> future time the action of the Spirit of truth who "convinces
> the world concerning the sin" of the rejection of Christ
> is linked inseparably with the witness to be borne to the
> Paschal Mystery: the mystery of the Crucified and Risen
> One. And in this link the same "convincing concerning
> sin" reveals its own salvific dimension. For it is a "con-
> vincing" that has as its purpose not merely the accusation
> of the world and still less its condemnation. Jesus Christ
> did not come into the world to judge it and condemn
> it but to save it (cf. Jn 3:17; 12:47). This is emphasized
> in this first discourse, when Peter exclaims: "Let all the
> house of Israel therefore know assuredly that God has
> made him both Lord and Christ, this Jesus whom you
> crucified" (Acts 2:36). And then, when those present ask

Peter and the Apostles: "Brethren, what shall we do?" this
is Peter's answer: "Repent, and be baptized every one
of you in the name of Jesus Christ for the forgiveness of
your sins; and you shall receive the gift of the Holy Spirit"
(Acts 2:37–38). In this way "convincing concerning sin"
becomes at the same time a convincing concerning the
remission of sins, in the power of the Holy Spirit. Peter
in his discourse in Jerusalem calls people to conversion, as
Jesus called his listeners to conversion at the beginning of
his messianic activity (cf. Mk 1:15). Conversion requires
convincing of sin; it includes the interior judgment of
the conscience, and this, being a proof of the action of the
Spirit of truth in man's inmost being, becomes at the same
time a new beginning of the bestowal of grace and love:
"Receive the Holy Spirit" (Jn 20:22). Thus in this "convincing concerning sin" we discover a double gift: the gift
of the truth of conscience and the gift of the certainty of
redemption. The Spirit of truth is the Counselor.[1]

In Peter's preaching, Peter confronts his listeners with the
truth. "This Jesus ... you crucified and killed by the hands
of lawless men." Peter states the unvarnished truth: "You
killed him." The Acts of the Apostles say: "Now when
they heard this they were cut to the heart, and said ...
'Brethren, what shall we do [in order to be saved]?'" (Acts
2:37). The Holy Father John Paul II shows in his encyclical how the Holy Spirit is at work. First he sends them an
insight into their own guilt, and he sends them remorse.
Only through the Holy Spirit can we have contrition. That
is why convincing by the Holy Spirit is something quite
different from what goes on in our world. It is not just a

[1] John Paul II, Encyclical *Dominum et vivificantem*, 31.

conviction, an exposure, but is meant to grant conversion, joy, and freedom. Only the Holy Spirit can do that, and he does it by awakening our conscience. The conscience, which reminds us what is bad and what is good, becomes the place of conversion. The Holy Spirit does not accuse, he does not just convict, but he also grants consolation and forgiveness, an assurance of mercy. Not without good reason does Jesus speak about the great, intense joy over conversion: "There will be more joy in heaven over one sinner who repents than over ninety-nine righteous persons who need no repentance." That is the difference: the world convinces and convicts by accusing. Just as the devil does according to the Book of Revelation: "who accuses them day and night" (Rev 12:10). The Holy Spirit turns souls away from sin and leads them into the joy of forgiveness. He puts our sins in the light of truth, so as to show the truth of mercy and forgiveness. We are still on the way; our pilgrim journey is not yet ended. We have not yet been led into all truth, all sin has not yet been exposed, all righteousness has not yet been accomplished. But wherever conversion has already begun, the joy of the Holy Spirit shines forth.

IX

"I Am with You Always,
to the Close of the Age"

On the Way to Our Final Destination

Peter once said to Jesus: "Behold, we have left everything and followed you. What then shall we have?" What will be our reward? Jesus tells him: "Truly, I say to you, in the new world, when the Son of man shall sit on his glorious throne, you who have followed me will also sit on twelve thrones, judging the twelve tribes of Israel. And every one who has left houses or brothers or sisters or father or mother or children or lands, for my name's sake, will receive a hundredfold, and inherit eternal life" (Mt 19:27–29). They are talking about the reward for discipleship. To pose the question quite objectively: Is discipleship worthwhile? Is it worth it to go to Jesus' school of life? As shocking as the question may sound at first, Jesus did not reject it. Jesus permits all our questions, even though we ourselves are often afraid to permit questions.

What is in it for us if we follow Jesus? Discipleship is very demanding, and so it is quite understandable that Peter once asked, on behalf of all the Twelve: "Is it worth it to give up so much in order to follow you?" For you have to give up a lot when you follow Jesus. Many find it demeaning to ask a question about a reward. It is supposedly much better to do good unselfishly and altruistically, without asking: What is in it for me? What do I get out of it? It is supposedly much better to do good for the sake of the good and not to ask about the reward. Jesus does not see things that way. In his discourses, in his preaching, he speaks very often about the reward. Maybe that simply comes from his professional life. He knows that the worker earns his wage. So he himself once said: "The laborer deserves his wages" (Lk 10:7). Therefore it is not forbidden at all to ask: What is the reward for discipleship?

Eternal Reward

Jesus gives a two-part answer: "There is no man who has left house or wife or brothers or parents or children, for the sake of the kingdom of God, who will not receive manifold more in this time, and in the age to come eternal life" (Lk 18:29–30). Eternal life—eternal reward.

Even though Jesus explains that discipleship, a life spent following him, bears much fruit already in this life, it is clear: the full reward will be eternal life. Discipleship therefore means much renunciation but also a great reward. This is stated clearly in the last, the eighth Beatitude: "Blessed are you when men revile you and persecute you and utter all kinds of evil against you falsely on my account. Rejoice and be glad, for your reward is great in heaven" (Mt 5:11–12).

A great reward in heaven is Jesus' promise again and again. This is the starting point for the old Marxist accusation, which the older ones among us used to hear: You console people with the afterlife but do not change this life. Instead of making this world more just, you console people with the next world, in which there will be justice. In the hereafter you will be happy. The point is that everyone is unhappy here. Karl Marx described this "hereafter consolation" of religion as "the opium of the people". Thereby people are anaesthetized so that they do not feel the pain of this world so much, so that they endure injustice and do not change this world.

What do discipleship and Jesus' school of life mean in this perspective of eternal life? Is the reward for discipleship only in the next world? To clarify this question from the outset: the reward for following Jesus consists neither of a paradise on earth nor of a paradise in heaven; rather, the reward consists of someone who is this fulfillment. Jesus is the reward. He is the fulfillment, he is "the way, and the truth, and the life" (Jn 14:6). Someone who experienced that very intensely was Paul. After he had encountered Christ, he said about himself: "To me to live is Christ, and to die is gain" (Phil 1:21). Paul is expressing a fundamental experience that we find again and again in the great figures of the Christian life:

> Yet which I shall choose I cannot tell. I am hard pressed between the two. My desire is to depart and be with Christ, for that is far better. But to remain in the flesh is more necessary on your account. Convinced of this, I know that I shall remain and continue with you all, for your progress and joy in the faith. (Phil 1:22–25)

Both options are good for Paul: to be here, as a sojourner (elsewhere he says, "in exile"), or to be at home with the

Lord. But it is better to be completely with the Lord. But that is possible only when we depart from this life, from this world, and leave the flesh, so as to be completely with the Lord. In the Second Letter to the Corinthians Paul expresses this dramatically:

> For we know that if the earthly tent we live in is destroyed, we have a building from God, a house not made with hands, eternal in the heavens. Here indeed we groan, and long to put on our heavenly dwelling, so that by putting it on we may not be found naked. For while we are still in this tent, we sigh with anxiety; not that we would be unclothed, but that we would be further clothed, so that what is mortal may be swallowed up by life. He who has prepared us for this very thing is God, who has given us the Spirit as a guarantee.
>
> So we are always of good courage; we know that while we are at home in the body we are away from the Lord, for we walk by faith, not by sight. We are of good courage, and we would rather be away from the body and at home with the Lord. So whether we are at home or away, we make it our aim to please him. (2 Cor 5:1–9)

We have no concept of heaven; we can only approximate it in images. Paul attempts that here. The first image that Paul uses is the metaphor of a tent and a dwelling. This life takes place in an earthly building, or rather a tent. Paul knows of what he speaks, since he was a tentmaker. We "pitch our tents" here on earth; in the next world an eternal dwelling awaits us, "a house not made with hands". That means that we are housed here temporarily. There we will find a lasting abode that God has prepared for us, a permanent house. Jesus speaks about the many "rooms" or "mansions" in his Father's house (cf. Jn 14:2), literally:

monai, in his Father's house there are many "abodes". Here we have no lasting abode but only a tent. There we have an everlasting abode. That is the first pair of images: tent and house.

Then Paul uses the image of clothing. He tries to describe the abode, and he mixes his metaphors. Alongside the image of the house not made by human hands appears the image of the clothing. Paul says that our present condition is, so to speak, a kind of "nakedness". We are as we are described at the beginning of the Bible, fallen human beings who "knew that they were naked" and were ashamed (Gen 3:7). That is the *conditio humana*, human life. Job, the sorely tried man, when everything is taken away from him, everything is destroyed, his family is dead and he is sick, says: "Naked I came from my mother's womb, and naked shall I return; the LORD gave, and the LORD has taken away; blessed be the name of the LORD" (Job 1:21). Paul speaks about eternal life no longer as being unclothed but, rather, as being "further clothed"; not about becoming naked again as at birth but, rather, about being clothed anew. The image is of eternal life as a garment that definitively covers our nakedness and ends our homelessness.

This brings us to a third pair of images, the polarity between being at home and being abroad. "While we are at home in the body we are away from the Lord." So Paul describes our earthly life. Living in the body, being "at home in the body", means literally that we "are abroad", not at home, away from the Lord, not abiding in the Lord. Therefore Paul would prefer to travel away from the body, or, to translate the Greek literally, to "leave home away from the body", so as to resettle with the Lord and to be at

home with the Lord. But then he says: It makes no difference, after all, whether he is at home or abroad—literally,
whether he abides with the Lord or away from him—it
is always about the Lord. He is intent on pleasing him.
Whether we are away, *here*, or at home, *there*, we seek to
please the Lord. It is always about him, the Lord.

Finally Paul uses a fourth pair of images (whereby
only one side of the metaphorical coin is presented), the
image of body and soul, which addresses the fundamental
reality of a human being: We are a unified composite, one
human being composed of body and soul. Paul does not
mention the soul explicitly as he does in other passages, but
he is thinking of it, for earthly life is life "in the body", he
says, or "in the flesh". Going home to the Lord is a departure from the body, so to speak, an exodus from the body.

Body and Soul

Many people have difficulty with the distinction between
body and soul. The Bible speaks only about the whole
human being, they say. Many fear that the distinction
between body and soul is not biblical but, rather, part of
the philosophical heritage, especially from Greek philosophy, which introduced the distinction between the material body and the spiritual soul.

Again and again the fear is expressed that distinguishing
body and soul could tear apart the unity of man. But distinguishing does not mean dividing. The Council, in the Pastoral Constitution on the Church in the Modern World,
speaks about man and says that he is *corpore et anima unus*,
"though made of body and soul, [he] is one" (*Gaudium et*

spes 14). What does that mean? The *Catechism* offers very clear words on this subject:

> The human person, created in the image of God, is a being at once corporeal and spiritual. The biblical account expresses this reality in symbolic language when it affirms that "then the Lᴏʀᴅ God formed man of dust from the ground, and breathed into his nostrils the breath of life; and man became a living being" (Gen 2:7). (*CCC* 362)

The whole man is therefore willed by God, but as an individual consisting of body and soul. When the Bible speaks about the soul, it very often simply means the whole man, the life of the man. Therefore in biblical translation the word "soul" is often translated into Greek as *psyche*, "life", and that is accurate in many cases. But the word "soul" also designates the innermost aspect of man. "For what doth it profit a man, if he gain the whole world and suffer the loss of his own soul?" (Mt 16:26, Douay-Rheims); this must be the correct translation of the verse: soul, not "life". The soul can suffer harm, and that is worse than when the body suffers harm. For the word *soul* designates what is most valuable in man. We see this in the martyrs, who are willing to lose their bodily life rather than to surrender their soul. "The soul" therefore signifies "the *spiritual principle* in man" (*CCC* 363).

The body shares in the dignity of being made in the image of God; it is a human body precisely because it is animated by the spiritual soul. Our bodies have much in common with the animal world; we are living beings and have a profound affinity with the whole plant and animal kingdoms. All that is part of us, but we are still animated by a spiritual soul, down to the innermost aspect of our body. That is why man as a whole is destined to become the temple of the Holy Spirit in the Body of Christ. "Do you not know that your body is a temple of the Holy Spirit ...?" (1 Cor 6:19).

Then the *Catechism* emphasizes the profound unity of body and soul. It is so deep that we have to regard the soul as the form of the body. The spirit-soul therefore causes the body, which consists of matter, to be a living human body. In man, spirit and matter are not two united natures, but, rather, their union forms a single nature. Perhaps it is most evident in psychosomatic medicine how thoroughly the spiritual and the corporeal mesh, the extent to which spiritual suffering is expressed in the body and vice versa. As the humorist Wilhelm Busch says about Balduin Bählamm, a caricature of an unhappy poet: "... and in the cavity of the molar dwells the soul." Because he has such a terrible toothache, everything in him now is toothache. This is the experience of the psychosomatic unity.

Even in the Old Testament the Bible is acquainted with body and soul. This becomes decisively clear in one of Jesus' sayings: "Do not fear those who kill the body but cannot kill the soul; rather fear him who can destroy both soul and body in hell" (Mt 10:28). In Judaism the distinction between body and soul is found especially in the texts of prayers, just as in Christianity. Therefore, when Paul says, "depart from the body", he also means bodily dying, death.

It implies no contempt for the body when Jesus admonishes us that we should not fear him who can kill the body; rather, it indicates that there is something more precious than bodily survival. Viktor Frankl put it memorably in his account of his experience in a concentration camp: "Those

who looked out only for their bodily survival were the first
to perish. Those who did not sell their soul often survived
in the body, too." The distinction between body and soul
is no doubt one of the essential components of Christian
anthropology, of the Christian and biblical teaching about
man. We have learned that death is the separation of body
and soul and that resurrection is the reunion of body and
soul in glorified human nature (cf. *CCC* 362–67). The loss
of this clear distinction leads also to a lot of helplessness; I
observe this especially in the whole field of death and dying.

Prayers for the Dying

The topic that Paul addresses—"departure from the body,
going home to the Lord"—was taken for granted for centuries in the Christian view of death. One German expression for "death, decease", *Heimgang*, literally means "going
home". I have the impression that the loss of the prayers
for the dying in the Church is the reason why today we
are so mute and helpless in the face of dying. We have no
formal expressions, no language, no rituals for it. What
Paul describes as a "homecoming from exile", the departure from the body and the entrance into our homeland
with the Lord, is elaborated wonderfully in the major texts
of the Christian liturgy for the dead. My favorite prayer
in this context is the so-called *commendatio animae*, the
commending of the soul as it goes home. It used to be
that many people knew this prayer by heart. My great-
grandmother always asked: Do you know the prayers for
the dying? She wanted to be sure that, when she died,
someone would be there who knew the prayers for the

dying by heart. I am afraid that nowadays hardly anyone knows them by heart; I do not. I will quote a few passages from this marvelous prayer, which according to Christian tradition is prayed at the moment of the soul's departure from the body and its return home, in order to show what became of the experiences of the apostle Paul in the great tradition of the Church:

Depart, O Christian soul, from this world,
in the Name of God the Father Almighty, who
   created you,
in the Name of Jesus Christ, Son of the living God,
   who redeemed you,
in the name of the Holy Spirit, who was poured out
   upon you.

Today may your dwelling place be
in peace with God on the holy Mount Zion,
with the Blessed Virgin Mary, Mother of God,
with Saint Joseph, and with all the angels and saints
   of God.

May you return to your Maker,
Who formed you from the mud of the earth.
May Blessed Mary, the angels, and all the saints
come forth to meet you as you depart from this life.
May you see your Redeemer face to face
And enjoy the contemplation of God for all eternity.
   Amen.[1]

---

[1] Cited in: Christoph Schönborn, *Existenz im Übergang* (Einsiedeln, 1987), 136–38.

The dying person is urged to set out, *depart*: Go home, it is time to let go! What a profound knowledge about the process of dying is contained in this prayer! Then the choirs of angels are mentioned, who come to meet the dying person on his return home to God's dwelling place. The dying person is therefore encouraged not to delay. Set out on the journey! Dying is a journey. Do not hesitate, do not delay, go in the name of God and of all the saints, depart from this world. This expresses the profound knowledge that this return home is a journey on which one must be accompanied by prayer. This is why formerly people were not allowed to die alone, and they were accompanied by prayer even beyond the moment of death, because the soul, after all, has quite a way to travel. Death is a departure on a long journey.

De hoc saecolo migrare iussisti—"You commanded us to travel out of this world", we read in this old prayer for the dying. Next come these wonderful commendations: "I commend you, dear Brother, to Almighty God, whose creature you are ... and if now your soul departs from the body, may the radiant host of angels hasten to meet you." I heard a testimony about a young Muslim who died at the age of eighteen—the nurse who was attending him told me this. As he was dying, he saw three angels who gestured to him. He asked his mother, who did not want to let him go, "See, the angels are coming! May I go?" Then she agreed that he could die. That is plainly an experience of what the prayer describes: "If now your soul departs from the body, may the radiant hosts of angels hasten to meet you." The prayer continues: "May peace surround you in the bosom of the patriarchs; may the Blessed Virgin Mary, the Mother of God, turn her eyes to you benevolently: may the face of Jesus Christ appear to you solemnly."

The *Commendatio animae* puts into words something of which all religions were aware but that we have forgotten to a great extent: the fact that the journey to the beyond is not without its dangers. It says in this prayer for the dying:

> May you not heed all that frightens in the
>   darkness....
> May the detestable Satan retreat from you
>   with his minions:
> May he tremble when you approach, accompanied
>   by the angels,
> and flee into the horrid chaos of eternal night....
> Thus may Christ, who died for you, free you from
>   everlasting death.
> May Christ, the Son of the living God,
> make you rest forever on the lovely green pastures
>   (*amoenia viventia*) of his paradise....
> May you behold your Redeemer face to face....

This is how Fra Angelico (d. 1455) depicted it,[2] based on the experience of this prayer, which was part of the common Christian heritage. How sad that we have lost this knowledge. How important it would be for an *ars moriendi*, the art of dying. People used to learn this, there were special books for it. How does one prepare oneself for death? How do you learn to die; how do we learn to depart from this world and go home?

[2] Fra Angelico, *The Last Judgment* (1432–1435), Museo San Marco, Florence; Fra Angelico, *The Last Judgment* (after 1439), Gemäldegalerie, Berlin.

Jesus says: The reward for discipleship is eternal life. Paul shows that yearning for Christ is the real object of hope for eternal life—not just any continued existence, but rather the encounter with Christ, the endless state of being with him and in him. Even the yearning for eternal life takes its measure from Christ. We just saw, however, that this very love for Christ, in other words, discipleship in practice, teaches Paul the true relation between the yearning to return home to Christ and the duty to stay here in exile, so as to serve Christ in his brothers and sisters. Therefore, if we want Paul to show us what the goal of discipleship is, we must look for a moment at what it meant for him to remain here for the love of Christ and to take upon himself all the efforts of discipleship.

I imagine Saint Paul as being rather short, incredibly lively, and strong. I personally have experienced him in a new way as a brother in the Lord and have found such vitality in reading his letters that I can only be grateful for it. I am thinking of one passage in the Second Letter to the Corinthians where Paul speaks about the labors of his apostolic ministry and also about his sufferings and about conflicts within the Church. These have always existed, and they were by no means any smaller than the ones today. The unbelievable tension between the followers of James, about whom James himself incidentally says: "We gave them no instruction" [cf. Acts 15:23–29], but who want to be "more Jacobite" than James, or "more Catholic than the Pope". We have that nowadays, too. James, on the one side; Paul and Barnabas, on the other. Think of all that Paul had to suffer and endure! In the Second Letter

to the Corinthians he gives free reign to his heart for once
and says:

> Whatever any one dares to boast of—I am speaking as a
> fool—I also dare to boast of that. Are they Hebrews? So
> am I. Are they Israelites? So am I. Are they descendants
> of Abraham? So am I. Are they servants of Christ? I am a
> better one—I am talking like a madman—with far greater
> labors, far more imprisonments, with countless beatings,
> and often near death. Five times I have received at the
> hands of the Jews the forty lashes less one. Three times
> I have been beaten with rods; once I was stoned. Three
> times I have been shipwrecked; a night and a day I have
> been adrift at sea; on frequent journeys, in danger from
> rivers, danger from robbers, danger from my own people,
> danger from Gentiles, danger in the city, danger in the wil-
> derness, danger at sea, danger from false brethren; in toil
> and hardship, through many a sleepless night, in hunger
> and thirst, often without food, in cold and exposure. And,
> apart from other things, there is the daily pressure upon
> me of my anxiety for all the churches. Who is weak, and I
> am not weak? Who is made to fall, and I am not indignant?
>
> If I must boast, I will boast of the things that show
> my weakness. The God and Father of the Lord Jesus, he
> who is blessed for ever, knows that I do not lie. (2 Cor
> 11:21b–31)

What ardent words from Paul! How much his discipleship cost him! He endured it all because the love of Christ
impelled him. When I read passages like this, I have to
say: My God, what are my difficulties in comparison
to this incredible total commitment of the apostle! Why
does he put himself through all of that? He himself gives

the answer: "For the love of Christ urges us on, because we are convinced that one has died for all; therefore all have died. And he died for all, that those who live might live no longer for themselves but for him who for their sake died and was raised" (2 Cor 5:14–15). Paul does not fear death. For him dying is gain, we heard him say, returning home to Christ. But neither does he flee from the labors of his ministry. Because for him life was Christ and dying—gain.

Light and Shadows

"What will our reward be?" Peter wanted to know that. Jesus' answer includes both: present and future. It shows that the afterlife is by no means just a consolation prize for those who suffer here. I will cite the passage that I quoted at the beginning from Matthew, but now from Mark, who has a somewhat different version:

> There is no one who has left house or brothers or sisters or mother or father or children or lands, for my sake and for the gospel, who will not receive a hundredfold now in this time, houses and brothers and sisters and mothers and children and lands, with persecutions, and in the age to come eternal life. (Mk 10:29–30)

The reward for discipleship is a hundredfold even now— persecution included, of course. A hundred times as many brothers, sisters, mothers, children, and so on, and even lands and houses. I do not mean that ironically now, when I think of the many buildings to be main- tained in the Archdiocese of Vienna, but truly. In how many houses are we at home, because we have brothers and sisters in the faith throughout the world. Precisely at a time when the weaknesses, errors, and sins that have never been lacking in the Church have come to light and are being highlighted in a particular way, it is important not to become fixated on them. In the Vatican, at all levels, there are excellent men who are serving the local Churches quietly and patiently; they are true examples. There is also mediocrity, which is a danger to us all and which we have here in Austria likewise, and also really bad things, as there always are where sinful human beings are at work. So it is with the Church as a whole. Light and shadows, sin and sanctity. But the light has always prevailed. There has always been a genuine counterbalancing holiness. I know from many personal encounters that there are real saints in the Roman Curia. Many, many people who work honestly and also suffer painfully amid the failings. The Church's life has always been stronger than the destructive forces.

"Look not on our sins, but on the faith of your Church", we pray the Lord at every Eucharist. Let us, too, look at the faith of his Church, at the people in whom faith shines, and then we will not be scandalized by the wounds and sins of the Church, as sad and painful as they are.

Impossible for Men, but Possible for God

I conclude these meditations on Jesus' school of life with two apparently quite contradictory words and deeds of Jesus. These two references should help us to look wistfully at our own efforts on behalf of discipleship and, at

the same time, to see that only the Lord can really make
us disciples.

The first saying shows us how difficult, indeed, how
humanly impossible it is to reach the goal of discipleship
fully by ourselves. Someone asked Jesus, " 'Lord, will those
who are saved be few?' And he said to them, 'Strive to
enter by the narrow door; for many, I tell you, will seek
to enter and will not be able' " (Lk 13:23–24). Who reaches
the goal? Is this saying of Jesus about the narrow door only
"for others", "for those outside"? Or is he saying it to us?
Is it so difficult only for the others to come through the
narrow door, to enter into life, or is it also and perhaps
especially difficult for the disciples? Whoever thinks that
it applies only to others should listen to another saying of
Jesus. When Jesus saw the rich young man go away sad,
unwilling on account of his wealth to follow Jesus, then
Jesus uttered the serious saying about the camel and the
needle's eye: "It is easier for a camel to go through the eye
of a needle than for a rich man to enter the kingdom of
God." This caused great alarm among the disciples: "Who
then can be saved?" If discipleship is that difficult, who then
can ever reach the goal? Salvation, heaven? Jesus looked
at them and told them: "With men this is impossible, but
with God all things are possible" (Mt 19:24–26).

Humanly impossible—we are called to set out on a path
to a goal about which we are told: We cannot possibly
attain it on our own. Discipleship is not possible by our
own efforts. Yet that means: discipleship is possible only
with Jesus and only through him, and not as my own life
plan with my virtues, with the list of virtues that I set out
to practice. And certainly not with Christian values about
which people constantly speak today. Only as the result of

"living with Christ" and "being with Christ" can we be disciples. He alone can make us his disciples. Everything that we may contribute, all our striving to come through the narrow door of discipleship, is already his grace that is drawing us.

In order to make that clear, let us mention the first disciple who reached the goal, to whom the Lord first gave the reward of discipleship, eternal life:

> One of the criminals who were hanged railed at him, saying, "Are you not the Christ? Save yourself and us!" But the other rebuked him, saying, "Do you not fear God, since you are under the same sentence of condemnation? And we indeed justly; for we are receiving the due reward of our deeds; but this man has done nothing wrong." And he said, "Jesus, remember me when you come in your kingly power." And he said to him, "Truly, I say to you, today you will be with me in Paradise." (Lk 23:39–43)

The "thief on the right", a criminal who in the last moments of his life became a disciple of Jesus, is the first one who received the reward about which Peter asked and that Jesus promised: "eternal life". A strange "patron saint" for Jesus' school of disciples, but quite after the heart of him who said that in the kingdom of heaven there will be "more joy ... over one sinner who repents than over ninety-nine righteous persons who need no repentance" (Lk 15:7). So we ask this good patron, Saint Dismas, that we, too, may reach the goal of discipleship.

SCRIPTURE INDEX

Genesis

1:31	125
2:7	146
3:5	88
3:7	144

Exodus

33:11	66

Leviticus

11:44	69
19:2	69

Deuteronomy

18:15	66
34:10	66

Job

1:21	144

Psalms

22:2	56
51:4	87
69:33	105
127:1	13

Proverbs

25:21	73

Isaiah

6:5	82
43:1	32
54:13	38
55:8	14
62:5	79

Jeremiah

15:16	111
20:7	23

Hosea

11:1	50

Matthew

1:21	80
2:15	50
4:19	22
4:23	46
5—7	60—75
5:1—2	62
5:4—5	71
5:11—12	141
5:13—14	64
5:20	78
5:21—22	64
5:22	41
5:25—26	77
5:27—28	64

Matthew (continued)

5:29–30	41
5:37	41
5:42	41
5:43–45	72
5:48	38, 74, 78
6:1	64
6:25–26	65
6:25–26, 34	74
6:34	74
6:45	38
7:24–25	61, 74
7:28–29	65, 111
8:10	78
8:20	72
9:9–13	76
9:37–38	39
10:16	92
10:28	147
10:32	122
11:20–24	55
11:25	113
11:25–27	55
11:28–29	72
11:29	15
13:52	46
14:15	131
15:28	132
16:16–17	55
16:17	20
16:18	20
16:19	20
16:21–23	21
16:23	14, 19

16:24	30, 91, 93
16:24–25	24
16:25	25
16:26	82, 146
19:21	69
19:24–26	156
19:27–29	140
23:8	37
24:12–13	90
25:1–12	77
25:31–46	42
26:27–28	83
26:36–46	101
26:39	101
28:18–20	107
28:19–20	15
28:20	108, 123, 124, 127

Mark

1:14–15	46
1:15	17, 39, 138
1:17	31
1:18	31
1:24	82
1:35	47
2:1–12	81
2:5	81
2:14	39
3:1–6	132
3:13–15	31
3:21	36
3:32	36
9:32	92

10:29–30	154	23:55—24:1	40
12:41–44	42	24:46–49	122
14:71	24		
15:34	56	*John*	
		1:1, 18	53, 66
Luke		1:17	65
1:77	80	1:18	66
1:79	79	1:29	80, 90
2:46, 48–49	50	1:38	44
5:8	82	1:38–39	53
6:12–17	54	1:39	45
7:9	132	1:48	78
8:1–3	40	3:17	137
9:18–20	54	6:45	38
9:23	102	6:67–68	9
9:51	92	10:10	15
10:3	92	12:21	45
10:7	141	12:47	137
11:1	48	13:13–14	36
12:58–59	77	14:2	143
13:23–24	156	14:6	15, 126, 142
15:7	77, 79, 157	14:18	127
15:10	79	14:26	124, 127
15:31	21	15:8	15
18:29–30	141	15:9–11	132
19:1–10	39	15:9, 11	15
19:41	78	15:13	98
22:19	34	15:15	126
22:60–62	83	15:16	32
22:61–62	100	15:16a	20
23:34	56, 87	15:20	92
23:39–43	157	15:26	127
23:46	56	16:8	90, 128
23:49	40	16:8–11	136

John (continued)

16:12	126	
17:1–26	20	
17:21–22	35	
20:22	138	

Acts of the Apostles

1:8	122
2:36	137
2:37	138
2:37–38	138
4:13	34, 112
4:20	112
5:42	111
9:4	99
15:23–29	152
22:3	35

Romans

5:10	74
6:17	115
8:26	57
8:26–27	57
8:32	126

1 Corinthians

1:9	38
1:22–23	93
1:23	99
4:9–13	71
5:7	130
6:19	147
7:17	38
9:1	99

9:27	102
11:23	108
13:9, 12	125
15:3–5	121
15:11	121

2 Corinthians

4:8–10	71
5:1–9	143
5:14–15	103, 154
6:8–10	71
11:21b–31	153

Galatians

1:14	99
1:16	99
2:20	99, 103
5:11	99
5:22	133
6:12	99

Philippians

1:21	99, 142
1:22–25	142
2:5	100
2:6–11	101
3:17	100
3:18–19	100

Colossians

1:13	79

1 John

2:20–27	118

James

2:16   74

I Peter

1:8–9   133

Revelation

2:4   89

12:10   139

21:5   18, 125